DELIGHTS
OF THE
GARDEN

Vegetarian Cuisine Prepared Without Heat from Delights of the Garden Restaurants

Main Street Books

DOUBLEDAY

NEW YORK   LONDON   TORONTO

SYDNEY   AUCKLAND

DELIGHTS

OF THE

GARDEN

IMAR HUTCHINS

A MAIN STREET BOOK
PUBLISHED BY DOUBLEDAY
a division of Bantam Doubleday Dell Publishing Group, Inc.
1540 Broadway, New York, New York 10036

MAIN STREET BOOKS, DOUBLEDAY, and the portrayal of a building
with a tree are trademarks of Doubleday,
a division of Bantam Doubleday Dell Publishing Group, Inc.

Book design by Marysarah Quinn

Library of Congress Cataloging-in-Publication Data
Hutchins, Imar.
Delights of the garden : vegetarian cuisine prepared without heat from
Delights of the Garden restaurants / Imar Hutchins. — 1st Doubleday ed.
        p.   cm.
Rev. ed. of: The joy of not cooking / Imar Hutchins, editor. 1994.
Includes index.
1. Vegetarian cookery.   2. Raw foods.   3. Nutrition.   4. Delights
of the Garden (Restaurant)   I. Delights of the Garden (Restaurant)
II. Title.   III. Title: Joy of not cooking.
TX837.H88   1996
641.5′636 dc—20   95-26016
                                                                      CIP
ISBN 0-385-47965-4
First Main Street Books Edition: May 1996

1   3   5   7   9   10   8   6   4   2

To the memory of Dana and Stacy
—whose spirits are now guiding us.

To: Mom & Dad

Acknowledgments

Dawn Daniels. She saw the potential of the project. Made my hard-headed self see it too. *And* selflessly made it happen.

Denise Stinson. My agent. She patiently and confidently guided me into, what are for me, uncharted literary waters.

Bruce Tracy. My editor at Doubleday. To use his words, he's "so pumped" about this project. He gives it all the loving care it needs.

The people who made the earlier editions of this book a reality:

Robert Hinds, Rhonda Jordan, Isha Price, Tracy McQuirter, Sam Tucker

The Founders of Delights of the Garden

Anu, Ayize, Prince, Derrick, Joel, Mak, Steve, Kip, Andal

The people helping to take "Delights" to the next level: Susan, Marty, and Larry

And to all the true Grisslers out there.

CONTENTS

DELIGHTS

OF THE

GARDEN

INTRODUCTION

People are tired of the "health craze."

What America wants and needs is a healthy-living revolution. Today we find ourselves on the verge of just such a change.

We don't want more "diets" because to "diet" means to suffer—to do without. For those of us who like food and like to eat, why should we have to give that up?

Not eating animals is an idea that many of us have entertained in various ways and at various times. We've heard and read that a vegetarian diet is the best thing for us. To be honest, we find the notion of eating a dead, mutilated animal quite disgusting. But eating meat is such a part of our life. Hamburgers and hot dogs *define* American culture. Every time we've tried to become vegetarians it has only lasted a short while. Or maybe we have never even gotten around to trying.

Those of us who become vegetarians almost certainly look and feel better. However, many go back to our old diets before long because we feel like we're missing something. Scientifically it's proven that we're not missing anything nutritionally. The *taste* is what we miss!

Delights of the Garden wants to show the world that healthy diets can, and indeed should, taste good! Let Delights be your support group.

I often describe the creation of Delights of the Garden by saying:

"We all lived together and just kind of ended up eating this way." When my housemates and I at Morehouse College in Atlanta first eliminated heat from the preparation of the vegetarian foods we ate, we had no idea we were starting a phenomenon. Some of us had been vegetarians for years. Others of us were just getting into more healthy diets and life-styles.

We basically created a new cuisine by trying to eat things the way nature intended. We did our own nutritional research and experimentation in the kitchen. Through drawing on existing recipes and old-fashioned trial and error we came up with one new dish after another. All of our friends came to know and enjoy the food we prepared. As word spread around campus and around the city, we realized that a restaurant was a necessity.

Delights of the Garden is a young restaurant. It first opened in January 1993 in downtown Atlanta. Delights of the Garden advocates a new concept in healthful eating and living. Our menu is a unique diet of dishes made with totally noncooked fruits, vegetables, grains, nuts, and seeds for complete nutrition. Scientific research has shown that this diet is the most beneficial to the mind and body.

Delights of the Garden has been received excellently everywhere we've gone. Since the opening of our first restaurant in Atlanta, we've opened several restaurants in other cities. Many of our friends in various parts of the country and the world have wanted Delights of the Garden to come to their hometown. Many people have also been interested in owning their own Delights. Until now we have not been able to accommodate either of these requests. However, we are now laying the foundation necessary for large-scale expansion. People interested in owning a Delights of the Garden themselves will soon have that opportunity as we begin to sell franchises. We will also soon be selling prepackaged Delights of the Garden desserts in hundreds of health food stores and gourmet stores, first on the East Coast and ultimately nationwide.

Whether there's a restaurant in your city or not, let *Delights of the Garden* be your companion on your journey toward a healthy diet.

Some questioned our wisdom. "Why come out with a book giving away all of your secret recipes?" they asked. The answer is simple: we don't believe in secret recipes. Our goal is optimum health for as many people as possible. Educating people about how they can best take care of themselves is part of reaching that goal.

Don't feel that you've got to become a raw-vegetarian overnight —or ever, for that matter. Just relax and learn to listen to your body. Then give it what it asks for from you. Our bodies are constantly talking to us; we just usually don't listen—we don't know how to listen.

Begin by taking the Delights of the Garden Thirty-Day Good Health Challenge. Stop eating all meat for thirty days and discover how good you feel. You don't have to stop eating cooked food, just *all* meat (chicken and fish too)!

With *Delights of the Garden* as your guide, you'll have a full repertoire of recipes for great food. If you honestly don't feel better at the end of those thirty days, then go back to whatever diet you previously had. I'm sure, however, that if you're honest with yourself, then you will acknowledge that you feel much better. You will have more energy and vitality. You'll sleep better and may even lose weight. And, if you're eating dishes detailed in this book, you'll be discovering whole new kinds of tastes that you never even knew existed.

Come on. Let's see what *Delights* is all about!

THE PSYCHOLOGY OF NUTRITION

MILK. DOES IT DO YOUR BODY GOOD?

The consumption of dairy products is clearly one of the most illogical dietary habits. We are the *only* animal that consumes the breast milk of another animal! Not only that, but we also continue drinking this product in various forms all of our lives, while in nature a mother's milk is a source of nourishment only until the animal can digest its normal diet.

The milk from any mother (human, cow, dog, etc.) is designed to meet the special dietary needs of the young for that particular species. Cow's milk is designed for the dietary needs of a calf, not a human. During the first few months after birth, a calf's body weight increases at a rate several times that of a human baby, whose brain develops faster than its physical structure. In addition, cow's milk, as does human milk, contains an element called casein that is responsible for the physical development of a baby. Casein is found in a much greater amount in cow's milk than in human milk. Since most of us are not trying to raise 500-pound children, the use of cow's milk prevents our babies from receiving the necessary tools for proper brain development. The fact that dairy products also increase the amount of mucus in our bodies, which makes us more susceptible to illness, is one reason our children can often be seen with runny noses and are so highly prone to colds and ear infections.

By now many of you are probably having flashbacks of those commercials that say how important milk is for strong bones and teeth because of its calcium content. Calcium is indeed a very important element. Without it, our bodies would not be able to metabolize iron, which is important for the development of red blood cells. Milk, however, is not the best source of calcium. Calcium can also be found in kale greens, broccoli, oranges, sesame seeds, and unrefined grains. Many people feel like they would have to eat a barrel of kale or broccoli to get enough calcium. This could not be further from the truth. A serving of broccoli has more calcium than a glass of milk. If you find that surprising, kale greens actually have more calcium than broccoli.

"Steak" Just Sounds Better Than "Carcass"

As you move toward a more healthy life-style, it is important that you understand the psychology of meat-eating. To do this we have to remove all of the mental barriers that have been constructed in an effort to desensitize people to the thought of going to a supermarket and paying money for what is actually a carcass. What we call a thing is an indication of our mental attitude toward that thing. If some word has a negative connotation, more than likely people will have a negative attitude toward anything associated with it. This is the case with the term "vegetarian."

Vegetarianism gained popularity in this country during the late sixties and seventies when people were rebelling against the status quo. For this reason, many people have come to feel that vegetarians are spacey or weird. It is this type of stereotyping that has kept the meat industry in a profitable position.

Humans are social animals and have an innate desire to belong or be a part of a group. We want to be seen as "normal" or be a part of the "mainstream." Vegetarianism has come to mean something abnormal. As a result, many people shun the idea of a diet that does not include meat, because they do not want to be radically different from other people even if it is in their own best interest.

Language has also been used in ways less subtle. Because the term "meat" has come to represent the finished product that we consume, we do not make the association between "meat" and decaying flesh. This association is quickly made when the term "carcass" is used, although all three terms refer to the same thing. Likewise, we have come to refer to particular types of meat in ways that don't tell what they really are. For example, there was a commercial that told us that hamburger was chopped steak. What is steak? People do not want to call meat by the part of the body it comes from because that would bring the idea of a dismembered animal to the forefront of their minds. How many meat-eaters would volunteer to visit a slaughterhouse to witness for themselves the harsh reality that the animals experience each and every day?

We also want to point out the fact that most of us do not even think of dead chickens, turkeys, or fish when someone speaks of meat. As you may imagine, this is extremely profitable for the companies which sell these animals. Although eating chickens, turkeys, and fish is practiced by some people making the transition from meat-eating to vegetarianism, this book does not recommend the long-term consumption of fish and fowl because there is no one particular type of decaying flesh that is less harmful than any other.

Out of Sight, Out of Mind

Many of us have pets at home that we love dearly and would probably think it would be quite cruel, almost barbaric, if someone were to eat them. However, we are less uncomfortable with the idea of eating animals we seldom come in contact with alive.

Most people have never seen a slaughterhouse. This is because slaughterhouses are placed in isolated, rural areas so that we don't have to smell the stench and hear the dreadful screams of hundreds of animals awaiting their unnecessary slaughter. From a mental standpoint, we no longer associate the meat we eat with an animal that was once alive and capable of feelings. How many of us get hungry when we see cows grazing? Probably not as many of us who begin to salivate when a fast food commercial comes on television. Few of us would be able to witness the atrocities that take place in a slaughterhouse without reevaluating our food choices.

Make It Look Good

Our culture places incredible emphasis on how a thing looks. Whenever someone tells us about a person they've met, we immediately want to know how this person looks. When we are in the market for a new car, our final decision is often not based upon the quality of

the car and its record of reliability, but upon how it looks and how we will look in the car. A trip to your local supermarket is another good illustration of this fact.

Marketing experts understand quite well that how something looks will have a tremendous effect on the success of the product. Consequently, their job has become to make things look good, even if these things are detrimental to your health. If an attractive packaging can be developed, people will be attracted to the product because, for most people, appearance is our primary or only method of determining what we will put in our grocery carts. Should the USDA one day decide to require the meat and dairy industry to list the items that were fed to the cows, chickens, pigs, and turkeys on the packaging, the number of vegetarians in this country would certainly increase.

You're Your Own Boss

Some of us do not realize how important our food choices really are. Whatever you place in your body directly affects your health. Our medical experts would have us believe that it is all right to eat things not intended for human consumption as long as one eats them in moderation. We tend to disagree with that point. If decreasing the amount of meat and chemicalized foods reduces your chances of acquiring cancer and other diseases, it would be best for our doctors to advise us to adopt a diet that contained none of these items. We have to understand, however, that our medical industry is not one based on prevention. It is centered around drugs and surgery for treatment once an illness has been contracted. This is a very important reason why we do not receive the best nutritional information. In order for the health care industry to maintain its profitable status, it cannot deal with disease from a preventive standpoint. It is just that simple. In fact, most of us believe that it is more sensible to allow someone to cut open our bodies than to make some preventive changes in our life-style. Throughout this book and at our restaurant, however, you will find a wealth of preventive information and recipes that are part of a preventive life-style. We really enjoy seeing people making a move toward a healthier way of life. So if you have any questions, please come by one of our locations and we will be happy to talk with you.

What's Wrong with Eating Meat?

Vegetarianism and Planet Earth

Few of us consider the environmental consequences of a meat-based diet, but it has a great effect on the only planet we humans can call home. The effect is greater than merely the loss of millions of animals killed for food.

The destiny of the human race is inextricably linked to that of every other living thing on this earth—plant or animal. Inevitably, the destruction of one leads to the deterioration of the others, as we are presently witnessing. Current trends around the world illustrate that a meat-based diet causes meat companies to convert fertile farmland into areas for raising livestock.

Land is much less productive when used to raise livestock than to grow food for vegetarians. The use of farmland to grow animals for food is nowhere felt more than in the third world. For example, in Costa Rica, beef production quadrupled between 1960 and 1980, but most Costa Rican beef is exported to the United States. Today, much of the country's original tropical rain forest has been sacrificed to beef production. These facts may seem insignificant; however, if Americans reduced their meat consumption by 10 percent, enough grain would be saved to feed 60 million people.[1]

This phenomenon is not limited to Costa Rica. All over the world, countries that were once self-sufficient with regard to grain production are now dependent on foreign nations. In China, Mexico, and North and Northeast Africa, increases in grain-fed livestock require more imported feed. More and more land is used to grow livestock feed and to graze livestock. Economics forces even more people off their land. Since 1960, the number of landless people in Central America has multiplied fourfold.[2] International lending agencies such as the World Bank have given billions of dollars in loans to the livestock industry, which benefits the wealthy and undoubtedly worsens the situation for the general population. It should be clear at this point that a meat-based diet has severely detrimental effects from a global perspective, but what about from a personal standpoint?

A Little Closer to Home

We have come to believe that we need a great deal of protein. Is this belief valid? Objective authorities say no. The World Health Organization, the Food and Nutrition Board of the National Academy of Sciences, and the National Research Council say that, at the maxi-

1. Resenburger, B., "Curb on U.S. Waste Urged to Help World's Hungry," *New York Times,* October 25, 1974.
2. Ibid.

mum, we need only 8 percent of our total daily calories from protein.[3] According to Dr. David Reuben, a "safety" factor of an extra 30 percent was used to obtain this figure. This nutrition expert states that using this extra 30 percent only raises the income of people who sell meat, fish, cheese, eggs, chicken, and all of the other high prestige and expensive sources of protein.

The misinformation goes even further. The media has created the impression that the strongest person is the heavy meat-eater or the meat-and-potatoes person. A quick glance at the animal kingdom tells us otherwise. The strongest animals by far are not carnivores. They are vegetarians and fruitarians. Who is the giant of the animal kingdom? The lion may be the most brutal and ferocious, as are most carnivores, but it is not the giant. The real giant is the elephant, which eats fruits, leaves, and young branches. Even if we look at those animals which biologists have found to be quite similar to us physiologically, we will find vegetarians. The gorilla is not an animal to be taken lightly—its diet: ripe fruits and vegetables!

Meat Is a Secondhand Source of Protein

A complete list of all of the animals humans consume will no doubt consist of vegetarian animals like cows, chickens, and turkeys. This should help us to understand that the person who consumes animal

3. Scrimshaw, N., "An Analysis of Past and Present Recommended Dietary Allowances for Protein in Health and Disease," *New England Journal of Medicine,* January 22, 1976: 200; Irwin, M., "A Conspectus of Research on Protein Requirement of Man," *Journal of Nutrition* (1975); 101:385 and Hegsted, M., "Minimum Protein Requirements of Adults," *American Journal of Clinical Nutrition* (1968) 21:3520.

flesh is actually getting secondhand fruits, vegetables, and grains. These animals have built their bodies on a vegetarian diet which becomes mixed with the poisons within the carcass.

This problem is even greater when the animals come from slaughterhouses. As in humans, a sudden terrifying experience sends a rush of adrenaline, which is toxic, throughout the animal's body. Under normal conditions, this toxin would be diluted instantly by the bloodstream. However, between the time of the killing and the death of the cells and tissues, activity is still going on. When the heart ceases to beat, the diluting process stops and the poisons begin to accumulate. With all of the death that we consume daily, is it any wonder so many of us develop cancers and other terminal diseases?

The fact that meat is actually secondhand protein is quite obvious when you consider our conventional beliefs about meat. If meat were truly necessary for size and muscle, you would think that cows would eat it. What is really important for building our bodies are the amino acids.

Amino acids are made up of carbon, hydrogen, oxygen, and nitrogen atoms, and when these elements are combined in various ways they make protein. The protein in the animals we consume has been obtained from the raw foods they eat, which makes it pure protein. As humans eat animal flesh, our bodies must break down the protein from the form in which it was usable to the animal all the way down to the original atoms before we can begin building up protein that we can use. This eventually takes its toll on the human body and reveals itself through rapid aging and fatigue.

In order to dispel completely the idea that we need protein we can take an example from Mother Nature to illustrate our protein needs. I think we can all agree that milk from a healthy mother is basically nature's perfect food for an individual that is growing faster

than they ever will again. A human mother's milk provides 5 percent of its calories as protein. Nature seems to be telling us that even when our protein needs are greatest, we only need a small amount of our food calories as protein.

The meat and dairy industries have been playing mind games with us to increase their profits. It was almost inevitable that we would buy their sales pitch. After all, when we went to elementary school and learned the Four Food Groups from our teachers, we thought this information was being provided for our best interest.

OSTEOPOROSIS AND THE PROTEIN CONNECTION

The personal health consequences of a meat-based diet are astonishing. One quarter of sixty-five-year-old women in the United States have bone mineral losses so severe that the condition is given the clinical name "osteoporosis."[4] This condition results when a person has lost 50 to 75 percent of the original bone material from her skeleton. Because of the propaganda put forth by the dairy industry, we would naturally assume that these women were not taking in enough calcium. The National Dairy Council has spent a great deal of money selling milk as the solution. However, many research teams, working independently, have studied the effect of low and high protein diets on calcium balance and their studies have shown two things: (1) low

4. Solomon, L., "Osteoporosis and Fracture of the Femoral Neck in the South African Bantu, *Journal of Bone and Joint Surgery,* (1968) 50B:2; McDougall, J., *McDougall's Medicine,* Piscataway, N.J.: New Century, 1985, pp. 61–96. Linkswiler, J., "Calcium Retention . . . as Affected by Level of Protein and of Calcium Intake," Transcripts of the New York Academy of Science (1974) 36:333.

protein diets create a positive calcium balance, meaning bones are not losing calcium; and (2) high protein diets create a negative calcium balance, meaning osteoporosis is developing.[5] A high-calcium vegetarian diet is a good decision for women concerned about osteoporosis.

No Meat for the Herbivores, Please

There are generally three classifications of eating habits: herbivores, carnivores, and omnivores. Herbivores have a diet of fruits, vegetables, grains, and other nonmeat items. Carnivores, like lions and buzzards, eat other animals. They exist exclusively on a diet of dead animals. A carnivorous diet, even for carnivores, does not make for a long life relative to other animals. The last classification, omnivores (bears), eat everything. These types of animals, however, are naturally able to consume both plants and animals. Humans behave like omnivores, eating everything from delicious salads to decaying meat; however, it is not our natural diet based upon our physical makeup. A comparison of the anatomy of carnivores with that of humans (herbivores) clearly shows that we are not designed to consume meat.

Carnivores have specially designed teeth called canines and razor-sharp claws for tearing into flesh and ripping it off of the bone. Although human beings have fingernails and teeth classified as canines, they are in no way capable of tearing through the thick hide of an animal, assuming we could get close enough to it to try. Instead, we are

5. Ibid.

forced to use extensions of ourselves (i.e., spears, guns, etc.) to kill our food. The use of these weapons is merely a result of our inability to coexist with the natural order of things.

Second, the mouth is the first organ of the digestive system and a great deal takes place before the food continues its journey through the digestive system. As food is being chewed, it is mixed with saliva, which contains certain chemicals to aid in the breakdown of the food. Different kinds of foods require different chemicals. Carnivores have the necessary chemicals in their saliva to break down not only flesh but bones as well, whereas humans do not. If you were to take a piece of meat and place it in your mouth, it would probably remain indefinitely. However, an apple would gradually begin to soften because our mouths are equipped with the proper chemicals to break down fruits and vegetables and other nonmeat foods. We also lack the proper amount of acid and certain enzymes necessary to eat the flesh and bones of uncooked cows and turkeys. Because of this, we are forced to go through the elaborate ritual of washing the meat, adding flavorings to it, and placing it over a tremendous amount of heat. Every other meat-eating animal consumes the flesh as is. Some may argue that cooking is one of the benefits of technology. But just because the human mind can conceive something does not mean that it is the best for us.

Another characteristic of carnivores is their relatively short digestive system. The reason for this is that meat decays rapidly and creates a great deal of waste matter. The animal must be able to eliminate waste material quickly, otherwise, as we see in people, all sorts of diseases will occur. When we examine the human digestive tract, it measures over 30 feet. Our long digestive tract is designed for a fibrous diet and one that does not allow waste to settle along the way. Once again, the medical industry has given us only half of the information. They have told us to incorporate more fiber in our diets. What sense does it make to do this if you are going to continue to consume things that will remain in your system? Eating meat defeats the purpose of a diet high in nutritious fiber.

By eating a vegetarian diet, not only do you benefit yourself, but the effects of a plant-based diet are felt worldwide. Don't stop with this brief overview of nutrition. Talk to other people and continue to make yourself aware through vegetarian magazines and books of the benefits of a healthier life-style and ways to make the transition at a comfortable pace. In the next chapter, you'll learn what makes Delights of the Garden different from any other vegetarian restaurant.

WHY WE DON'T COOK

Traditionally, the term "cooked" has meant heating food to at least 120 to 140 degrees Fahrenheit for a given amount of time before consuming. This process should actually be called "killing." If we set any other item over such heat or fire for even a short period of time, we would undoubtedly do considerable damage. Why then, would it be any different with food? When something burns, it begins the process of breaking down, and eventually ashes form. The moment we apply heat to food this process begins, as we can so clearly see with food that has been cooked longer than intended. Food that has not been killed is food cooked to perfection. The sun and the earth provide all of the energy and nutrients that the food needs to reach its own natural state of perfection.

The benefits of enzymes are another important reason for not killing food. Enzymes are chemicals present in food which allow reactions to occur in our bodies and contribute to the breakdown of the food in the intestines. The enzymes present in whole (unprocessed, unrefined) foods are intact. However, heat destroys these enzymes and this forces the body to work extremely hard to digest the food and assimilate the nutrients into the blood stream. At Delights of the Garden we understand the importance of obtaining the full nutritional value from food, which is why we are here to offer you a complete menu of uncooked and unrefined foods.

In regards to our health, even introducing live foods as a part of your diet will certainly bring about drastic improvements. You will begin to consume less food because more nutrients would be available to the body. All of those pounds that have been overburdening our bodies will begin to melt away. A proper diet also helps to rid the body of many ailments we think our genes have complete control over. Problems like high blood pressure, high cholesterol, arteriosclerosis, ulcers, skin problems, asthma, allergies, and obesity would soon disappear. Our bodies will, in time, be rejuvenated and we will be able to get the full benefits of life.

It has been researched and demonstrated for years that a diet consisting of fruits, vegetables, whole grains, seeds, and nuts is the optimum diet for human beings.

Perhaps the most obvious reason for advocating a live food diet is quite simple. Cooking is totally unnecessary. Cooking is probably the reason most of us eat so many processed, refined foods that only require reheating in a microwave (which magnifies the harmful effects of cooking, not to mention the unknown long-term effects of that type of radiation). The most nutritious food can be prepared quickly and easily without going through the chore of cooking. Why would anyone choose to put in a full day of cooking for only one meal when you could easily prepare a meal for a few or many in a fraction of that time.

RAW FOOD VEGETARIANS ABROAD

As we look to cultures outside of our own, the benefits of a diet consisting largely of live foods are clearly evident. The Hunza people are

some of the most extensively studied vegetarians. They have become world-renowned for being among the healthiest, longest-living people in the world. These people do not suffer from many of the diseases that other people face. Such a high standard of living can only be attributed to their active life-style, positive mental attitude toward life, and a sound diet consisting of about *70 percent raw fruits and vegetables.* Heat damages foods; eating them in their natural state must be the perfect diet to nourish our perfect machines.

In recent years, we have seen the move toward energy conservation take place in industry as well as in individual households. The threat of cancer-causing air and water pollution, not to mention the potentially devastating deterioration of the ozone layer has everyone considering new ways to decrease energy use. So much energy is wasted by cooking that the practice of not cooking would have numerous benefits for the environment as well as our health. Common sense tells us that if we eliminated cooking, our energy costs would decrease while the energy obtained from the food would soar to its maximum potential.

The Thirty-Day Good Health Challenge

Some of the facts to which you have just been exposed may make you feel uncomfortable or may seem somewhat unbelievable. That is to be expected because the Four Basic Food Groups have been our standard of nutrition since the days when we sat in our elementary school classrooms. We only ask that you bring to this book and our restaurant an open mind.

If you want to experience a change in your own health, eliminate all of the unhealthy items from your diet (especially those for which you have strong cravings) for thirty days and we guarantee you will feel the difference. Some of you might be thinking you would be crazy not to eat animal flesh, animal by-products, or any other of your favorite foods for thirty days. But think about it. Thirty days is a very short period of your life. You really don't have much to lose. If you try a healthy life-style for thirty days and you discover how much better you feel and realize how we really live to eat, rather than eat to live, you will have given yourself another opportunity to get the most from life. Not only that, but you will be on the road to controlling all of those food addictions that now have control over you. If you look at it in this way, it is really a no-lose situation—but you will never know for yourself until you make the decision to at least try it. What do you have to lose? Absolutely nothing!

DELIGHTS IN YOUR KITCHEN

We pride ourselves on the simplicity of preparing our foods. You will, however, need some kitchen equipment to create our recipes at home. You may already have what you need. At the very least you'll want to have a good food processor and blender, you also may want to add a juicer and dehydrator for a few dishes.

Some recipes call for ingredients with which you may not be familiar. All ingredients required are relatively easy to come by and can be found in one of three places: a health food store, oriental grocery, or Middle Eastern market.

INGREDIENTS TO GET FROM AN ORIENTAL GROCERY:
Sesame oil
Seaweed (hijiki and wakame)
Dried layer seaweed
Miso (organic sweet white)
Tamari (similar to soy sauce)

INGREDIENTS TO GET FROM A MIDDLE EASTERN MARKET:
Cracked bulgur wheat (kush)
Tahini

Ingredients to Get From a Health Food Store:
Soy milk
Kelp (regular or powder)
Salt substitute
Raw honey
Pure maple syrup

Many recipes call for tamari, which is a soy-based sauce almost identical to soy sauce. The two can actually be used interchangeably. (The main difference is what is sold as "soy sauce" often contains alcohol as a preservative and sugar; tamari should not.) Certain products, such as Bragg's Liquid Amino's, can be substituted for tamari or soy sauce. The benefit in using such a product is that it is lower in sodium and provides just as good seasoning. It tends, however, to be rather expensive.

You will note that some recipes call for honey. Some vegetarians do not use any honey because they consider it an animal by-product. You can decide for yourself. If you do not wish to use honey, you can substitute maple syrup in most cases. If you do use honey, we suggest raw honey.

Although no recipes require cooking, some recipes call for heated water. We allow this because we define cooking as applying enough temperature to destroy the nutrients in the food. People argue about the temperature at which this occurs, but it's somewhere around 115 degrees Fahrenheit. The use of hot water does not significantly affect the nutritive value of food. You can use hot water you get from a teapot or coffeemaker, or—if you happen to live in the only place on the planet that still has clean water—from the tap.

RECIPES

Menu Foundations

Straight off the Delights of the Garden menu! You'll see that there's nothing on the menu that we don't teach you how to make—no secret recipes. Dishes in this section are the first things you should learn how to make because many of them form the basis for entrées and other recipes.

KUSH

1 cup dry kush (cracked bulgur wheat)
$1/2$ teaspoon garlic powder
$1/4$ teaspoon curry powder
2 tablespoons tamari (or soy sauce)
1 cup spring water
1 tablespoon extra virgin cold pressed olive oil
1 medium green bell pepper, diced
$1/4$ small red onion, diced
1 medium carrot, shredded

Put the dry kush in a mixing bowl and add the spices. Next cut the tamari into the mixture with a large spoon. Then add the water. You should be adding just enough water to provide about a $1/4$-inch layer of water atop the kush. Stir well and mat down the mixture evenly so that the kush will be evenly soaked. Cover and let sit for 25 to 30 minutes. After soaking, add the oil and stir. Then add the vegetables and stir again.

Now that the kush is complete, taste it. You may wish to add some more tamari. Also feel free to add any more vegetables you wish—tomatoes are especially popular.

SERVES 4 (ABOUT 3 CUPS).

Note: Using hot water allows the kush to be made more quickly. However, kush made with hot water should be refrigerated if not being served immediately because it will spoil more quickly than that made using cold water.

One's kush-making ability is the measure of one's skill in Delight's kitchen. A rookie's kush, for example, may come out too dry (crunchy, nutty tasting) or too wet (chunky and heavy). These mistakes can easily happen, so don't be frustrated, kush-making takes practice! There are countless variations of kush in this book, including spicy, curry, and jambalaya. You can find kush or "cracked bulgur wheat" in the bulk bins of any good health food store.

Before you begin, a couple of kush-making tips: remember that you can always add more water—you can't take it away. It's better to put in too little when you initially soak the kush. Then you can add more if you find it to be too dry. The same goes for the oil and tamari—you can always add more. Be sure to taste the kush every step of the way (every time you add something).

This recipe is for the basic form of kush, which serves as a basis for several other recipes that appear later.

Have you always thought that there must be something you can do with all of the carrot pulp that stays in the juicer after you juice carrots. Some make carrot cake, but you don't want to go from healthy carrots to unhealthy carrot cake; so what can you do? Here is a recipe for a dish that is delicious, yet healthy, and uses that carrot pulp. Veggie tuna. The name comes from its tunalike texture. The taste—DELICIOUS!

VEGGIE TUNA

5 pounds carrots, peeled
2 stalks celery
1 bell pepper, chopped (optional)
1 small red onion, diced
1 large tomato
1/2 cup Eggless Mayonnaise (page 46—also available in some health food stores)
2 tablespoons tamari (or soy sauce)
1 tablespoon sea salt or other salt substitute
2 teaspoons kelp seasoning

Juice the carrots in an electric juicer. Save the pulp to make this dish and enjoy the juice as a refreshing beverage. Finely chop the celery, bell pepper, onion, and tomato. Add the pulp of the carrots to the chopped vegetables. Knead the eggless mayonnaise into the carrot pulp mixture. Next knead in the tamari. Finally, knead in the sea salt and kelp seasoning.

SERVES 4 (3-4 CUPS).

NUTMEAT

1 large tomato
1½ cups sunflower seeds or nuts of your choice
2 cups completed Kush (page 29)
1 tablespoon chili powder
¾ cup Delights Natural Bar-Be-Que Sauce (page 119)

First puree the tomato in a food processor. Clean the food processor and then, using the "S" blade, finely chop the sunflower seeds or nuts. In a large bowl, combine the kush with the chopped sunflower seeds. Add the chili powder and stir together with a large spoon. Finally cut the sauce and pureed tomato into the kush-seed mixture.

SERVES 4 (4-5 CUPS).

Note: For those of you avoiding the high fat content of nuts, we make our nutmeat without even actually using nuts.

Yes, you have read correctly—a "nutmeat" made from cracked bulgur wheat, sunflower seeds, and a natural barbeque sauce. It's just the thing for those of you who love barbeque. You don't have to give up on your favorite tastes to be healthy.

Avocado Grand

5 ripe avocados
1 large tomato, chopped into large chunks
1 small red onion, diced
1 garlic clove, finely chopped
2 tablespoons tamari (or soy sauce)
juice of 1 lemon

Halve each avocado. Remove the seeds (pits), skins, and stems. Cut the avocado into $1/2$-inch chunks. Combine all the ingredients in a large bowl. Stir with a large spoon, mashing the avocado slightly as you go. Continue until it's the desired consistency. The lemon juice is an important ingredient, especially if you are not serving immediately. It will preserve the avocado. Otherwise avocado tends to discolor *very* quickly.

SERVES 4.

Marinated Veggies

1 head cauliflower, cut into bite-sized chunks
1 cup broccoli florets
5 carrots, cut into $1/4$-inch slices
1 red bell pepper, cut into $1/4$-inch strips
1 green bell pepper, cut into $1/4$-inch strips
1 small red onion, diced
1 tablespoon Italian seasoning
$1/4$ cup tamari (or soy sauce)
$1/3$ cup olive oil (extra virgin, cold pressed, preferably)

In a large bowl, mix all the veggies. Stir. Add the Italian seasoning and stir again. Add the tamari and stir. Add the olive oil and stir again. Refrigerate, covered, for 1 hour for optimum flavor.

SERVES 4.

So you think vegetables are best cooked boiled or steamed? If you do eat them raw, they are usually covered with cheese or a high-calorie dressing. Otherwise, they just don't taste as good. Why not try our recipe for marinated vegetables using simple spices, one of which is tamari. These raw vegetables also maintain their freshness and health content because they have not been killed by heat; they have not been cooked twice but cooked only once—and that was by nature's hot plate, the sun!

For those who know what hummus is you will enjoy preparing it in its truest form—raw—without being boiled. The taste is still delicious and the flavor even stronger. For those who are new to the hummus scene, this is undoubtedly something that you should prepare. Made with chick-peas, garlic, and lemon juice, this dish is perfect for party dips. You can use banana chips, carrot sticks, or anything you wish to dip in the hummus.

HUMMUS

1 1/2 cups dried chick-peas (garbanzo beans)
3/8 cup tahini
3 garlic cloves, chopped
1 tablespoon tamari (or soy sauce)
juice of 3 lemons
1/4 cup olive oil

First soak the chick-peas in water for 24 hours. This is very important. If you soak them for less than 24 hours they will probably still be very hard. Ready your food processor with the "S" blade. Process the chick-peas for about a minute. With the processor still running add the tahini, followed by the chopped garlic. (You must chop the garlic before you put it in the food processor. If you don't you may end up with chunks of garlic.) Now add the tamari, lemon juice, and olive oil. Finally, process for a couple minutes more. Hummus may require up to 10 minutes in the food processor. It is important that a homogenous pastelike consistency is achieved.

SERVES 2-4.

Seaweed Noodles

1 cup hot spring water
$^1/_3$ bag (about 3 cups) of wakame seaweed
1 tomato, chopped
1 red bell pepper, diced
$^1/_2$ small red onion, diced
1 tablespoon olive oil

First heat the water in a teakettle. Next, place the seaweed in a small bowl and add water. Depending on the exact seaweed you have, you may be adding more or less water than the recipe states. You should be adding just enough to hydrate (or dampen) the seaweed. Turn the seaweed to achieve an evenly dampened texture. Allow the seaweed to soak for 5 to 10 minutes. All of the water should be absorbed by the seaweed. If you add too much water, the natural flavor of the seaweed will be lost.

Next, cut the moist seaweed on a cutting board into 2-inch strips and place them in a bowl. Add the other ingredients to the bowl and mix well.

SERVES 4 (ABOUT 2 CUPS).

So you like noodles? Well, you'll really love our version of noodles— seaweed noodles no less! Okay, it doesn't taste like noodles, but it has a noodlelike consistency. A lot of people have trouble with the concept of eating seaweed, but once you try it you'll wonder why it took you so long to try it.

Wakame seaweed is available in most oriental markets and grocery stores. While many health food stores carry seaweed sheets, few carry this kind of seaweed, which is not flat but comes in long dry strands.

This is a new addition to the menu concocted by the chefs at the Georgia Avenue store. If you like broccoli, you'll love this. The tahini gives the dish a cheeselike kind of taste—thus we dubbed it primavera.

BROCCOLI PRIMAVERA

3 bunches of broccoli
$1/3$ cup tahini
1 garlic clove
$1/4$ cup lemon juice
$1/3$ cup spring water
2 teaspoons tamari (or soy sauce) or salt substitute (optional)
$1/2$ cup chopped mushrooms
$1/2$ cup sunflower seeds
$1/4$ red onion, chopped

Cut broccoli florets from the stalks and place the florets in a large mixing bowl. Next, blend the tahini, garlic, lemon juice, water, and tamari or salt substitute, if using, until smooth and creamy. Pour the mixture onto the broccoli florets and mushrooms and stir until evenly covered with sauce. Sprinkle in the sunflower seeds and onion. Stir again.

SERVES 4 (2-3 CUPS).

SWEET AND SOUR NUTMEAT

Yet another variation in the nutmeat theme—to me this is the *funkiest!* The Sweet 'n' Sour Sauce will make or break this recipe, so put a lot of care into making that.

1 cup sunflower seeds or almonds
1 ½ cups completed Kush (page 29)
½ red onion, finely chopped
1 green bell pepper, finely chopped
1–1 ½ cups Sweet 'n' Sour Sauce, as desired (page 121)

First, finely grind sunflower seeds or nuts in a food processor using the "S" blade. Mix the kush with sunflower seeds or almonds in a blue tub. Add the onion and pepper. Add the sauce a little at a time. Should not be too moist nor too dry. Should resemble meat loaf.

SERVES 4 (ABOUT 4 CUPS).

This salad is really a more elaborate version of the Seaweed Noodles (page 35). That's why it's not included in the Salads section. If you have time and feel like experimenting, try this for a real adventure in taste and texture.

MA-NE NET SEAWEED SALAD

3 cups dried wakame seaweed
$1/2$ sweet red bell pepper, chopped
$1/2$ cup chopped red onion
$1 1/2$ red tomatoes, chopped
$1/8$ teaspoon cayenne
$1/2$ teaspoon onion powder
$1/2$ teaspoon garlic powder
$1/8$ teaspoon dry mustard
pinch of sea salt or other salt substitute
1 tablespoon sesame oil
1 tablespoon olive oil
1 tablespoon tamari (or soy sauce)
1 tablespoon raw honey or maple syrup

In a large bowl, add just enough hot spring water to the seaweed to cover it. Allow this to sit for 5 to 6 minutes, until the seaweed has absorbed most of the water and has a green-leafy consistency. Squeeze the remainder of the liquid out of the greens. Add the chopped vegetables and mix well. To this mixture add the dry ingredients and again mix well until the spices are evenly distributed. Following this add the remainder of the ingredients. Mix well and serve.

SERVES 4.

BABA GANOUSH

1 large eggplant, chopped
1 cup tahini (or soy sauce)
6 garlic cloves
1/2 cup olive oil
1 teaspoon salt substitute
1 tablespoon parsley flakes

Puree all the ingredients in a food processor until they're creamy.
Try serving with banana chips. Combining baba ganoush and
Hummus (page 34) is also a great dish.

SERVES 4.

If you like the Hummus
you're sure to love the
baba ganoush. It's our
variation on another
Middle Eastern staple. This
time the base is eggplant
instead of chick-peas. It's
great as a dip. Try it also
as a spread.

Okay, no more of that canned sweet corn off the cob. Or that horribly nasty corn salad in a can from the supermarket. It's time to start buying it by the ear (husk and all). I'm talking about walking into the kitchen (knee high by the Fourth of July/straight out of the cornfield), ripping off that husk, cutting up those kernels, and with a few dices and spices you'll run that jolly green guy right out of the cabinet.

CORN HUSKER

4 ears of corn, shucked, silks removed
1 red bell pepper, chopped
1 tomato, chopped
$1/2$ red onion, diced
pinch of red pepper flakes
4 teaspoons curry powder
3 teaspoons chili powder
2 teaspoons salt substitute
$1/4$ cup sesame oil

Don't cook the corn; cut the kernels off of the cob raw. In a large bowl, combine the corn with all the vegetables and mix. Add the spices. Stir again. Add the oil. Stir thoroughly.

SERVES 4 (ABOUT 2 CUPS).

TABOULI

1 cup dry kush (cracked bulgur wheat)
1/2 teaspoon garlic powder
1/2 cup spring water
1/4 small red onion, chopped
6 sprigs of fresh parsley, chopped
1 tablespoon tamari (or soy sauce)
1 tablespoon extra virgin cold pressed olive oil
2 tomatoes, chopped
2 teaspoons fennel seed

In a mixing bowl, combine the dried kush and garlic powder. Add the water and let the kush soak for 10 to 20 minutes, or until soft. Add the onion, parsley, tamari, olive oil, and tomatoes. Mix well. Add the lemon juice and mix well, then add the fennel seed.

SERVES 4.

Tabouli is an uncooked vegetarian dish that you may already know. It's a staple food in the Middle East. But of course you have not really had tabouli until you've tried ours. It's mild and fresh tasting—perfect for dinner on a summer evening.

MARINATED BROCCOLI

There are so many who love broccoli—and there are also many ways to prepare it. However, it can never be wrong to try something new. This dish has sort of an oriental flair to it. The sesame oil dominates. Combined with the little zip of the green and red bell peppers and the zap of the onion—it adds a whole new dimension to the preparation of broccoli.

3 bunches of broccoli, florets only
1 red bell pepper, finely chopped
1 green bell pepper, diced
$^1/_2$ red onion, diced
$^1/_2$ cup sesame oil
2 tablespoons tamari (or soy sauce)

Place all the ingredients in a container that has a lid, adding the tamari and sesame oil last. Cover with the lid. Shake the mixture up like a tossed salad. Best if allowed to sit 30 to 45 minutes so that the flavors can marry. Serve on a bed of lettuce.

SERVES 4.

CURRIED NUTMEAT LOAF

This variation on the basic Nutmeat (page 31) is good for those of you who like a curry sort of flavor. It's one of those dishes that everybody likes, which makes it great for times when you're having some of your nonvegetarian friends over for dinner.

1 cup finely ground sunflower seeds or nuts of your choice
1 cup completed Kush (page 29)
$^1/_2$ large onion
2 garlic cloves
2 tablespoons curry powder
$^1/_3$ cup Delights Natural Bar-Be-Que Sauce (page 119)
2 tablespoons soy sauce
1 scallion
$^1/_4$ cup spring water
$^1/_2$ green bell pepper, chopped

In a large bowl, mix the sunflower seeds and kush together. Set aside. In a food processor, add the remaining ingredients to make the curry sauce. Pour onto the kush mixture and mix well. Should resemble meat loaf. (Please feel free to add more curry sauce if necessary.)

SERVES 4.

¡Ay Caramba! Hold on to your hats because Delights salsa will knock you right out of the kitchen and onto the dance floor. I've had many customers inquire as to what brand of salsa we use, and where they can get it. When I walked out to speak to them I found them doing the calypso, merengue, cha-cha, and more! Experiment with it and see for yourself. You can use it as a dip, sauce, or another ingredient, but whatever you do—remember, no dancing in the kitchen!

SALSA

4 tomatoes
1 green bell pepper
$1/2$ red onion
2 garlic cloves
2 teaspoons sea salt or salt substitute
2 teaspoons chili powder
1 teaspoon ground cumin
2 teaspoons Italian seasoning
1 teaspoon paprika (for color)

Cut the tomatoes in quarters and the pepper in half. Using a food processor with the "S" blade, add the tomatoes, pepper, onion, and garlic. Process on high for 45 seconds. Add the spices and process for another 30 seconds, until relatively smooth with only a few chunks remaining. Oh, the longer you let it sit—say, covered in your refrigerator—the better it gets. Try to let it sit for at least an hour. Great for dipping chips of your choice. Try with dehydrated banana chips.

SERVES 2-4.

CUCUMBER AND TOMATO DELIGHT

I know, I know, you love it! And when you taste it you'll love it even more. The combination of these two mislabeled fruits, along with a balsamic vinaigrette and fresh spices is sure to excite your tongue.

2 cucumbers
3 tomatoes
1 teaspoon sea salt or salt substitute
1 tablespoon Balsamic Vinaigrette (page 133)
1 teaspoon dried dillweed, or 1 tablespoon chopped fresh dill

If waxed, peel the cucumbers. Cut the cucumber along its length, rotate a quarter turn, and cut along the length again. At this point, when you chop the cucumber you should get 4 pieces with each chop. Chop the tomatoes in large chunks. Place the cucumbers and tomatoes in a bowl. Add the sea salt, vinaigrette, and dill. Stir well.

MAKES ABOUT 3 CUPS.

Veggie Tuna just isn't Veggie Tuna without our eggless mayonnaise. This magical mayonnaise has all the flavor of your favorite salad dressing and more. It's delicious. Try our eggless mayonnaise for your own favorite dishes. Notice that by making your own almond milk you can make the mayo soyless. If you feel a little more experimental, try the next recipe—Magnificent Mayo.

EGGLESS MAYONNAISE

1 cup raw almonds
$^{3}/_{4}$ cup spring water
1 tablespoon onion powder
1 teaspoon salt substitute
2 tablespoons raw honey (may substitute regular honey)
juice of 1 lemon
1 cup vegetable oil (corn, canola, safflower), as necessary

Make almond milk by combining the almonds with the spring water in a blender and liquefy the combination. The blender may have to run for several minutes. One cup of unflavored soy milk may be substituted for the almond milk.

In a food processor, add the almond milk or soy milk, onion powder, salt substitute, honey, and lemon juice. Process with the "S" blade or whisk attachment for 30 seconds. Slowly add the oil. The mixture will begin to thicken. Add oil slowly, *only* until mixture is the consistency of mayonnaise. Longer processing will result in thicker mayonnaise.

MAKES ABOUT 2 $^{1}/_{2}$ CUPS.

MAGNIFICENT MAYO

2 cups Brazil nuts
$^1/_8$ cup olive oil
$^1/_2$ cup spring water
$^1/_2$ cup fresh lemon juice
4 teaspoons tamari (or soy sauce) or salt substitute

In a food processor, process the nuts until they are a pastelike consistency. Slowly add all of the oil while the mixture is still processing, then add the water, lemon juice, and tamari until all of the mixture is emulsified.

MAKES 3 CUPS.

This is a heavier version of the mayonnaise because it's made with Brazil nuts. Try this mayo in the coleslaw recipes in the Salads section.

ENTRÉES

This section lists some of the most popular main dishes on our menu. Most of these dishes require foods that you must first learn how to make in the preceding "Menu Foundations" section.

Delights of the Garden Sampler

The Delights of the Garden Sampler is the perfect dish for first time delighters. The wonderful combination of dishes helps you to not just taste, but experience the wide range of flavors and palate pleasers that the Garden in your home has to offer. Fix a plate for your friends, they'll love you for it!

Kush, mild (page 29)
Nutmeat (page 31)
Veggie Tuna (page 30)
Avocado Grand (page 32)
Marinated Veggies (page 33)
Nori Rolls (page 109)

Fill a third to a half of a plate with kush. Using a small (2- to 3-ounce) ice cream–type scoop, place 2 scoops of nutmeat and 2 scoops of veggie tuna adjacent to the kush. Next, add a serving spoonful of avocado grand in the center of the plate and marinated veggies along the edge of the plate covering any of the plate that is still bare. Finally, line the kush with two nori rolls stuffed with kush.

SERVES 1.

So you have a hearty appetite and these vegetarian dishes just don't fill you up—or so you think. It's time for you to prepare the goulash. With the combination of avocado, nutmeat, and our tangy salsa on a bed of alfalfa sprouts, this is a surefire dish for the hungry eater.

GOULASH

2 large lettuce leaves
1 large avocado
Nutmeat (page 31)
Salsa (page 44)
alfalfa sprouts

First use the lettuce leaves to create a bed on the plate. Make sure that the lettuce is clean and attractive; you may want to let it protrude slightly from the perimeter of the plate. Next, slice the avocado in half and remove the pit and skin (be sure to also remove any remnants of the stem).

Cut half of the avocado into chunks and put them on the center of the plate. Now add 2 scoops of nutmeat and lightly cut the nutmeat into the avocado chunks using a knife. You want the combination to stay in the center of the plate and to rise at least $1^{1}/_{2}$ inches off the plate at this point. Next, add the other half of the avocado in chunks forming another layer, making the dish stand taller. Now add one more scoop of nutmeat atop what should be a small mountain by now. Finally, pour salsa over the top of the mountain and line the edge of the plate with alfalfa sprouts.

SERVES 1.

Un-Pizza

Crust

¹/₂ medium-sized tomato, chopped
¹/₂ cup sun-dried tomatoes, oil-packed or plain
¹/₂ cup ground almonds
I cup ground pumpkin seeds
¹/₄ teaspoon sea salt or salt substitute

Blend fresh and sun-dried tomatoes together in a food processor. Transfer to a bowl and combine well with the other ingredients until the consistency is doughy. Press the crust into a well-oiled 9-inch pie pan and dehydrate in a food dehydrator for 3 to 4 hours, or until the crust is firm. If an oven is used, heat to 200 degrees, cut oven off, and then place the crust in the oven with the door open.

Filling

25–30 sun-dried tomatoes
¹/₄ cup plus I tablespoon olive oil
2 tablespoons tamari (or soy sauce), to taste
2 tablespoons dried pizza seasoning
¹/₂ tablespoon Italian seasoning
3 medium yellow pan squash, shredded
3 medium zucchini, shredded
I small onion, chopped
2 tablespoons organic sweet white miso
I cup chopped pitted olives

Move over all you other pizzas, our unbelievable un-pizza is the greatest thing since pizza began. This feast is everything you want in flavor and taste without all the things your body doesn't want or need. No cheese to tie your body up in knots, just lots of love and great taste.

At least 1 day before making the pizza soak the sun-dried tomatoes in almost enough water to cover them. Then add about ¼ cup of the olive oil and 1 tablespoon of the tamari. Stir well and cover. It's best to let these tomatoes sit for 24 hours or more. When you're ready to make the pizza, pour off the liquid using a strainer and discard.

In a food processor, puree the sun-dried tomatoes until they are of the consistency of tomato paste. Add to this the pizza seasoning, Italian seasoning, remaining tamari, and olive oil, until all are well-blended. In a large bowl, add this mixture to the shredded vegetables along with miso and mix well. Fill mixture into your crust (see above), and top with the olives. Serve at room temperature.

SERVES 2-4.

MONIFA'S PHILLY CHILI

4 cups soaked Kush (page 29)
$1/2$ cup chili powder
1 tablespoon dried oregano
1 teaspoon dried sage
$1/2$ teaspoon cayenne
1 teaspoon onion powder
1 teaspoon garlic powder
$1/4$ cup honey
$1 1/2$ cups spring water
1 tablespoon sesame oil
1 cup olive oil
juice of 2 oranges
8 large tomatoes, chopped into large pieces
1 stalk celery, finely diced
2 large onions, cut into $1/4$-inch slices
2 large zucchini, thinly sliced
4 garlic cloves, chopped

And you thought Philadelphia was best known for its cheese and its steak. We couldn't just stand by and let the bad guys get all the glamour. This chili has got practically everything in it. We're giving it to you Philly style, and it's so large, it's stepping over anything in its way. Where will that leave the cheesesteak? Probably rooming with The Last Action Hero. Well, that's the breaks in the business. Who knows, maybe there will be a sequel.

In a large bowl, combine the kush with the seasonings and mix well. To this combination add the honey, water, oils, and orange juice. Mix well. Add the remainder of the ingredients, mix well, and serve.

SERVES 8-10.

Note: This dish is best after it has set for 2 to 3 hours in order for flavors to combine.

LARON'S UN-CHILI

Are you a Westerner at heart? Texas isn't really that far away. You can enjoy a nice bowl of chili anytime you wish. And this recipe is even simpler than the preceding one.

1 cup Nutmeat (page 31)
¼ cup Delights Natural Bar-Be-Que Sauce (page 119)
1 teaspoon chili powder
1 tablespoon chopped onion
2 tablespoons chopped tomatoes
1 teaspoon garlic powder
2 cups hot spring water

Combine the ingredients in a mixing bowl and serve immediately.

SERVES 2.

VEGGIE STEW MEDLEY

Talk about a medley—whenever you mix fresh vegetables and stew it without brewing it, it brings music to **my** ears. Maybe I'm a little bit biased, but if you're not careful, they'll have you humming a tune as well. For heaven's sake don't serve it to a large party. If that's the case you might as well call it an anthem.

1 large bunch of broccoli
1 head cauliflower
1 head white cabbage
3 large carrots
6 large tomatoes
1 large zucchini
2 large onions
15 spinach leaves
1 teaspoon garlic powder
1 teaspoon curry powder
Pinch of dry mustard
Pinch of dried oregano
Pinch of sea salt or salt substitute
$1/4$ cup olive oil
$1/4$ cup sesame oil
1 cup spring water
juice of 3 oranges
1 tablespoon honey
juice of 1 grapefruit
$1/4$ cup tamari (or soy sauce)

Cut all the vegetables into large chunks and place in a large bowl. To this mixture add the seasonings and mix well. Add the oils, then the remainder of the ingredients. This should marinate, covered and refrigerated, for 3 to 4 hours for the best taste.

This dish is a favorite because of its downright creativity. Who would've ever thought of making spaghetti out of sprouts? You love Italian food but hate the pork sausage and beef. You don't have to give up. There is a better way—sprout spaghetti. With our famous nutmeat balls, this dish of bean sprouts is spectacular! And topped with our tangy salsa, delicious!

SPROUT SPAGHETTI

mung bean sprouts
3/4–1 cup Nutmeat (page 31)
1 cup Salsa (page 44)

On a small plate place a handful of bean sprouts. Atop the sprouts, using a small ice cream–type scoop, place 3 (2- to 3-ounce) scoops of nutmeat. Pour salsa over the combination and serve.

SERVES 1.

MOUSSAKA MARINARA

3 eggplants
7 garlic cloves
3 cups extra virgin cold pressed olive oil
dehydrated banana chips
Marinara Sauce (page 120)
1/2 cup sliced Kalamata olives
5 large mushrooms, sliced

No cooking or meat needed to make this squash dish! This delicious blend of eggplant, banana chips, mushrooms, salsa, and olives challenges your senses and takes you on a delicious voyage that you will never forget! You may never want to come home!

Cut the eggplant into half-moon-shaped slices 1/4 to 3/8 inch thick. Next, finely chop the garlic and combine it with the olive oil in a wide flat pan (such as a brownie baking pan). Soak the eggplant slices in the olive oil mixture until the eggplant is thoroughly soaked. (There's really no such thing as soaking it too long, since the longer you soak it the better it tastes. Five minutes might be a minimum, but a couple of hours or even overnight would allow the flavors to marry better and lets the eggplant get limp, which makes it taste more exotic.)

While soaking the above, put your banana chips in a food processor with the "S" blade installed and finely chop them. When soaking is done, "bread" eggplant slices in the pulverized banana chips (by wiggling the slices around in a pan full of chips). Now you're ready to serve. On a plate, place the eggplant slices in an attractive arrangement and pour a tablespoon of marinara sauce over each slice. Top it off with several slices of Kalamata olives and a few slices of mushrooms.

SERVES 4-6.

Here is another way to enjoy the wonderful kush that you prepare. Just throw it all in the pot! That's right. In this dish, a various assortment of vegetables and fruits make it a dish you will love. So, come with us to New Orleans and prepare the Kush Jambalaya— everyone needs a little vacation.

ABASI'S KUSH JAMBALAYA

4 okra (raw!)
1 squash
1 zucchini
3 celery stalks
1 green bell pepper
2 tomatoes
1 tablespoon Cajun seasoning
1 teaspoon tamari (or soy sauce)
3 cups completed Kush (page 29)
1 cup alfalfa sprouts (optional)

Cut all the vegetables into $\frac{1}{2}$-inch cube chunks. Combine them with the kush and add the Cajun seasoning and tamari. Mix well and serve heaped high on the plate. Surround the mound with alfalfa sprouts, if you like.

SERVES 4.

CURRY KUSH FEAST

So you like the flavor of curry, but you don't care for the goat that usually comes with it. Just add some corn, lemons, tomatoes, and of course as much curry as you desire to your kush and you have a feast fit for a king or queen.

2 ears of corn
2 tomatoes
3 cups completed Kush (page 29)
juice of 2 lemons
1–2 tablespoons curry powder
1–2 tablespoons tamari (or soy sauce) as desired.

Shuck the corn, remove the silks, and cut off the kernels. Next, cut the tomatoes into 1/4-inch chunks. Add these to the kush in a large mixing bowl. Add the lemon juice, curry powder, and tamari. Mix all the ingredients well. Serve mounded high on a plate. Try putting a tomato stuffed with spicy kush in the center and lining the edge of the plate with alfalfa sprouts.

SERVES 4.

This variation of our regular kush is sure to set your tongue ablaze with its flavor. It's perfect for those of us who like it hot!!

Spicy Kush

3 cups completed Kush (page 29)
2 teaspoons paprika (for color)
$1/2$ teaspoon cayenne
$1/2$ teaspoon red pepper flakes
2 teaspoons tamari (or soy sauce)

Add all the ingredients to the completed kush in a mixing bowl. You can feel free to vary the ratios of spices to your desired level of spiciness. The paprika doesn't really have any flavor, but it makes the kush darker and more red—and psychologically, darker *is* spicier. It's a good idea to add the cayenne and pepper spices a little bit at a time so that you don't overdo it, because it really is spicy.

SERVES 4.

ORIENTAL-STYLE KUSH

Once you've mastered the basic kush-making technique, no doubt you'll want to branch out and try different versions of kush. Oriental-style kush is arguably the most creative variant of the basic kush. The exotic tastes of fresh ginger, sesame oil, scallions, and cilantro combine to make this a truly memorable main dish.

3 cups completed Kush made substituting sesame oil for olive oil (page 29)
1 teaspoon garlic powder
1 teaspoon curry powder
$^1/_2$ red onion, diced
2 scallions, finely chopped
1 green bell pepper, finely chopped
1 tablespoon chopped fresh cilantro
1 teaspoon finely chopped fresh ginger
$^2/_3$ cup bean sprouts

In a large mixing bowl, combine all the ingredients, adding the bean sprouts last, and mix well.

SERVES 4.

We went all the way across the Atlantic to find this flavor. No more plain ol' quiche. That boring spinach has got to go. It's time to take a break and go on an expedition in search of a quiche bursting with taste. The only place to find food rich in taste is one that is rich in culture. To the east, my friend.

KENYAN QUICHE

FILLING

3 cups Veggie Tuna (page 30)
1 cup Seaweed Noodles (page 35)
1 cup Corn Husker (page 40)
2 teaspoons Cajun seasoning
1 teaspoon chili powder

Combine all the ingredients in a large mixing bowl.

CRUST

2 cups sunflower seeds
1 cup raisins
$1/4$ cup tahini

Make a crust by combining the above ingredients in a food processor until smooth and homogenous, and pat the mixture into a pie pan with your hands. Add the filling to the crust in the pie pan. Cut and serve.

MAKES 1 PIE.

SALADS

When most people think vegetarian they think: "All I can eat is salads!?!" As you've already seen in the preceding sections, this is not true. There's lots more on the Delights of the Garden menu than salads. However, when we do make salads, you know they've got to be memorable! This section is full of delicious ideas. Some are quick and easy. Look for a subsection called "Quick Green Salads"—you can throw them together in a few minutes. Others—like some of the most popular entrée salads—are a little more involved.

DELIGHTS OF THE GARDEN SALAD

This is for all of you *nonbelievers* who don't think that a salad will fill you up. This huge salad definitely will. We like to make this salad with 3 different types of lettuce plus tomato, cucumber, nutmeat, yellow squash, zucchini, spinach, avocado, and even seaweed.

1 head lettuce (or an assortment)
2 handfuls spinach leaves, torn by hand
3 tomatoes
1 cucumber
1 yellow squash
1 zucchini
1 avocado, pitted and peeled
1–2 cups Nutmeat (page 31)
$\frac{1}{2}$ cup hijiki seaweed, cut into small pieces
1 cup alfalfa sprouts

First form a mound of the mixed lettuces and spinach. Cut the various vegetables and toss them together with the greens. Cut the avocado into small chunks and sprinkle it over the salad. Also sprinkle small chunks of nutmeat and hijiki seaweed over the salad. Line the perimeter of the plate with alfalfa sprouts. Serve with your choice of dressing (see Sauces).

SERVES 4.

Here is a variation for our seaweed noodles. Although these noodles are great alone, when you add extra tomatoes, avocado, alfalfa sprouts, and spinach, you will definitely be on an undersea adventure. Oh, and while you're down there, visit the city of Atlantis. I hear that the weather there is great all the time.

POSEIDON'S ADVENTURE

1 handful spinach leaves
1 head red leaf lettuce
2 cups Seaweed Noodles (page 35)
2 tomatoes, diced
1 avocado, pitted and peeled, and cut lengthwise into $1/4$-inch-thick slices
1 cup alfalfa sprouts

Combine the spinach and lettuce and use them to form a bed on the plate. In the center of the plate, form a mound of seaweed noodles. Adorn the salad with generous portions of tomato and avocado. Line the perimeter of the plate with alfalfa sprouts.

SERVES 4.

CARIBBEAN "POTATO" SALAD

8 apples
$^1/_2$ cup lemon juice
I stalk celery, finely chopped
I large red onion, sliced
I cup tahini
1–2 tablespoons tamari (or soy sauce) or salt substitute
I tablespoon garlic powder
I cup spring water
$^1/_2$ cup raisins

No, friends, we're not trying to get you to eat potatoes without cooking them. Even **we** wouldn't ask you to do that. Instead, what we're pretending is potatoes are really apples—how creative, right? This is a wonderfully delicious and unique recipe. Try it at summer picnics and cookouts.

Slice the apples and sprinkle with half of the lemon juice. Add the celery and onion to the apples. In a food processor, blend the tahini, remaining lemon juice, tamari, garlic powder, and water until smooth and creamy. Should be slightly thick, like ranch dressing. Pour over the apples and mix. Sprinkle with the raisins.

SERVES 6.

ETHIOPIAN DELIGHT

I used to **hate** okra, but that was before I tried it raw—it's delicious. I wondered why anybody would ever cook it. See what I mean with this unique green combination of alfalfa sprouts, mushrooms, garlic, okra, and more. It can really be a full meal!

1 head green or red leaf lettuce (or use combination of both)
1 cup chopped broccoli florets
1/2 cup chopped okra
2 tomatoes, chopped
1 red bell pepper, diced
1 cup alfalfa sprouts
1 cup chopped mushrooms
1/2 garlic clove, finely chopped

After washing all the vegetables, place the ingredients in a large bowl and toss together. Add salad dressing if desired, preferably homemade. I recommend you try it with the Tomato-Dill Dressing (page 127).

SERVES 4.

Waldorf Salad

2 handfuls spinach
1 head green leaf lettuce
3 Granny Smith apples, peeled and cored
2 stalks celery, sliced
1/2 cup raisins
1/3 cup chopped almonds
1/4 cup sunflower seeds

First shred the spinach and lettuce together in a bowl. Next, chop the apples into bite-sized chunks and toss them together with the spinach and lettuce. Now add the celery. Place the salad on a plate and sprinkle the raisins, almonds, and sunflower seeds. Great when served with Tofu–Peanut Butter Dressing (page 129).

SERVES 4.

This salad is a particular favorite of many that come to the restaurant. They are intrigued, as maybe you are, with the combination of spinach, lettuce, raisins, celery, apples, almonds, and sunflower seeds. This salad is delicious, as you will come to find when you try it. It may become a favorite salad of yours as it is a favorite salad for so many others!

Here's my secret salad. It's so good I could eat it all day. It's best to eat this out of a bowl instead of on a plate, because you need to be able to dig into it to really have fun eating it!

My Secret Favorite Salad

2 cups alfalfa sprouts
3/4 cup dry wakame seaweed
1 tomato, diced
1 avocado, diced
3/4 cup Tomato-Dill Dressing or to taste (page 127)

Make a huge mound of alfalfa sprouts—the whole bowl. Sprinkle lots of crinkly wakame seaweed on top, ripping it into small pieces as you go. Sprinkle chunks of tomato and avocado on top of it. I'm known for being a dressing freak. So the last step is to douse the salad with tomato-dill dressing—lots of it. Eat it with a fork— delicious.

SERVES 1.

ORIENTAL-STYLE ZUCCHINI

You don't always have to go to China to get some great food. All that is really needed is some zucchini, a bit of oil, and fresh ginger, and lastly some tamari sauce, and you will have a dish from the Orient with a twist— a "delight-ful" twist.

fresh ginger to taste
4 scallions
³⁄₄ cup sesame oil
1 tablespoon tamari (or soy sauce)
4 zucchini

Finely grate the ginger. Cut the scallions into very small slices. Combine the ginger, scallions, sesame oil, and tamari in a medium-sized mixing bowl. Cut the zucchini into slices about ¹⁄₈ inch thick. Cover and refrigerate for several hours, to allow the flavors to blend.

SERVES 2.

Although there's a lot more to Delights of the Garden than salads, if we do make a green salad then you better believe it's gonna be the best. This is a good side dish with any meal, cooked or raw. The balsamic vinaigrette dressing is essential. Don't cut corners by trying to use apple cider vinegar or any kind of vinegar other than balsamic. Take your time with the dressing and you can't go wrong.

GREEN DREAM SALAD

1 pound spinach, finely chopped
1 green bell pepper, chopped
1 zucchini, halved and sliced
1 stalk celery, chopped
$\frac{1}{2}$ red onion, chopped
Balsamic Vinaigrette to taste (page 133)

Combine the vegetables in a salad bowl. When ready to serve, add the balsamic dressing.

SERVES 4.

Note: This dish should *not* be swimming in balsamic dressing but should instead be barely coated.

MELONS WITH LIME

We would love for you to try your melons a new way. Our melons with lime is just the recipe for you. It's honeydew and cantaloupe made with limes to give them a unique flavor, while enhancing the flavor that both of these delicious fruits already possess.

3 tablespoons grated lemon peel
1 tablespoon honey
$^1/_2$ cup lime juice
2 cups honeydew melon balls
2 cups cantaloupe balls
mint leaves for garnish

In a small bowl, mix the lemon peel, honey, and lime juice. In a large bowl, add the mixture to the melon balls, cover well, and refrigerate for 2 hours. Use mint leaves for garnish before serving.

SERVES 2-4.

You may have never thought about preparing ambrosia without marshmallows and cream. But this is an ambrosia that is truly for the gods—without the cream, this ambrosia is wonderful because of its purity and steady stream of pure fruits. If you are a fruit lover, this ambrosia, as well as the tropical fruit salad, are two dishes that we know you will love!

AMBROSIA

I grapefruit, peeled and sectioned
$1/2$ cup crushed pineapple
I banana, cut into $1/4$-inch-thick slices
$1/4$ cup pitted cherries
I orange, peeled and sectioned
$1/2$ cup seedless grapes
$1/2$ cup sliced strawberries

In a large bowl, mix the ingredients together, chill, and serve in dessert cups.

SERVES 4-6.

Tropical Fruit Salad

Everyone loves fruit. So making a tropical fruit salad is great fun. It's delicious and beautiful as well. In fact, it usually looks so good you hate to eat it.... Well almost!

4 bananas, sliced
4 red apples, peeled and diced
3 green apples, peeled and diced
$1/4$ cup chopped figs
$1/4$ cup raisins
$1/2$ cup seedless grapes
3 pears, diced

In a large bowl, mix the ingredients and serve. For variation, top with honey, coconut flakes, or sunflower seeds. Chill before serving if desired.

Serves 4.

Quick Green Salads

The following is a collection of salads that are easy to make in a hurry but delicacies nonetheless. You can whip them up when you don't feel like doing a lot or when you just want a little something to fill up that empty corner in your stomach!

WHOLE MEAL SALAD

You need a salad that's not just a side salad, but a whole meal!?! That's not a problem! For a big salad that's easier to make than one of the granddaddy salads, this is your bet.

1 head red leaf lettuce
1 handful spinach leaves
1 cucumber or zucchini, cut into $^{1}/_{4}$-inch-thick slices
1 scallion, sliced
2 tomatoes, cut into chunks
1 yellow squash, cut into $^{1}/_{4}$-inch-thick slices
$^{1}/_{2}$ cup fresh alfalfa sprouts

Tear the lettuce and spinach leaves into bite-sized pieces and place in a large bowl. Add the cucumber or zucchini, scallion, tomatoes, and squash. Serve immediately with Creamy Tahini Dressing (page 131) or your own dressing.

SERVES 4.

This is a distinctive garden salad that doesn't require a whole lot of work to prepare. The sweetness of the raw corn combined with the coconut milk is scrumptious.

Garden Lover's Salad

½ cup fresh young sweet corn kernels
½ cup shredded and chopped crisp cabbage or lettuce
2 tablespoons onion, parsley, or other minced seasonings
2 tablespoons grated coconut, chopped peanuts or mixed nuts

Serve over the salad, sliced or chopped:

¼ cup tomato or cucumber
2 tablespoons coconut milk (optional)

Combine all the ingredients in a large salad bowl and toss together.

Serves 2.

ARTICHOKE SALAD

¹/₂ cup artichoke hearts, washed, cubed or chopped
1 tablespoon minced onion
¹/₄ cup flaked or chopped pine nuts or grated coconut

In a large bowl, mix all the ingredients well and serve.

SERVES 1.

I remember I used to think artichoke hearts were some kind of meat. Disgusting, people eating the **hearts** of some little animal?!? How wrong I was. Artichokes are a delicious **vegetable,** as you'll see with this easy-to-prepare salad for one.

There is more to salad than iceberg lettuce. Our spinach-mushroom salad is a perfect example of this. This salad is more than what you are used to. The spinach and mushrooms are a lethal combination that will have you rethinking what you think about salads.

Spinach- Mushroom Salad

2 handfuls spinach leaves
6 mushrooms
$1/2$ cup raw sunflower seeds

Shred the spinach and use it to form a mound on a plate. Slice the mushrooms and generously arrange them atop the spinach. Sprinkle the sunflower seeds over the salad and serve with Balsamic Vinaigrette (page 133) or Sunflower Dressing (page 128).

SERVES 4.

Simple Salad

This is a quick salad with a truly unique sweet and crunchy taste.

¹/₄ cup fresh young sweet corn or white corn kernels
¹/₄ cup chopped wax beans, green beans, or endive
2 tablespoons grated coconut
2 tablespoons finely chopped peanuts (optional)

Over the salad pour:

1 tablespoon each olive oil or honey

Combine all the salad ingredients in a bowl. Over the salad pour the olive oil and honey.

Serves 1.

Note: Add honey just before serving as it will harden if allowed to stand.

Discover the taste of shredded potato—raw! The cayenne gives it a little zip (or a lot of zip if you like). Mashed avocado makes it slightly creamy.

POTATO AND CARROT SALAD

1 carrot, grated
1 medium unpeeled potato, grated
1 teaspoon chopped onion
1 teaspoon olive oil
$1/2$ avocado, peeled and mashed
minced fresh parsley
cayenne and paprika to taste

In a bowl, mix all the ingredients together.

SERVES 1.

MIDSUMMER SALAD

This is supposed to make you think of summertime even if it's the dead of winter. The light and nutty combination makes a good meal on its own when you're in the right mood.

¹/₄ cup fresh young sweet corn kernels
¹/₄ cup shredded and chopped lettuce, endive, or cabbage
¹/₄ cup chopped peanuts or mixed nuts
1 tablespoon olive oil or honey
1 tomato, finely chopped

In a bowl, mix together the ingredients, and serve.

SERVES 1.

The perfect easy-to-prepare party food for you to bring on a potluck or to serve at a get-together.

FLYING SAUCERS

4 medium cucumbers, sliced
1 avocado, pitted and peeled
juice of 2 lemons
tamari (or soy sauce), salt substitute, or seasonings of your choice

Place a little spring water in the blender. At a low speed, add 3 of the sliced cucumbers, unpeeled unless nonorganic. Blend into a fine consistency. Work in the avocado and the lemon juice. Season to taste with tamari, salt substitute, or seasonings of choice. Place this mixture on the remaining cucumber slices or use as a dip.

SERVES 6 AS AN HORS D'OEUVRE.

Coleslaws

If you are a coleslaw lover, have we got good news for you! Introducing coleslaw—not one but six different recipes—that will "delight" your taste buds! Not only are these slaws delicious, but fantastically healthy because they are made with a special, eggless mayonnaise that you will really enjoy. You can make the eggless mayo from scratch from either almonds or soy milk. Add that to our outstanding mixtures of fruits or veggies and you have several masterpieces.

BASIC COLESLAW

1 pound carrots, peeled, grated
1/4–1/2 head red cabbage, sliced or grated
1 1/4 cups raisins
Eggless Mayonnaise (page 46) and honey to taste

In a medium-sized bowl, add the grated carrots, cabbage and raisins. Add the mayonnaise and honey. Stir well and serve.

MAKES ABOUT 2 QUARTS.

Complimenting Coleslaw

1 head green cabbage
1/2 head red cabbage
1 cup grated carrots
1 small purple onion, finely chopped
1 small stalk celery, chopped
1 medium sweet green bell pepper, chopped
1 medium sweet red bell pepper, chopped
2 medium scallions, finely chopped
4 teaspoons tamari (or soy sauce) or salt substitute or to taste
3 tablespoons fresh lemon juice
1/4 teaspoon paprika
1 teaspoon onion powder
1/4 teaspoon garlic powder
1/4 cup honey
1/4 cup Magnificent Mayo (page 47)
2 large tomatoes, chopped

Shred the green and red cabbage. In a large bowl, combine and add the grated cabbage. Add the onion, celery, chopped peppers, and scallions. Add all of the seasonings and mix well until the juices of the vegetables have blended well with the seasonings. Add the mayo and tomatoes last so that the tomatoes will not become too crushed. Mix well again.

SERVES 6-8.

Raisin-Carrot Coleslaw

1 head red cabbage
$^1/_2$ cup grated carrot
$^1/_2$ small purple onion, chopped
3 teaspoons sea salt or salt substitute
$^1/_4$ cup seedless raisins
2 tablespoons lemon juice
2 tablespoons honey
2 tablespoons Magnificent Mayo (page 47)

Shred the cabbage by use of a hand grater or food processor. Place into a large bowl along with the carrot and onion. Add the sea salt and mix well. Next add the raisins, lemon juice, honey, and mayo. Mix well and serve.

SERVES 6-8.

Pineapple-Apple Coleslaw

1 head red or green cabbage
$^1/_2$ fresh pineapple (ripened)
1 cup chopped peeled apples
$^1/_2$ cup chopped celery
3 tablespoons Magnificent Mayo (page 47)

In a large bowl, shred the cabbage. Peel and chop the pineapple, and add it along with the remaining ingredients. Mix well.

SERVES 6.

GRATED CARROT SALAD

4 cups grated carrots
$1/4$ cup raisins
$1/4$ cup crushed pineapple (fresh or canned)
$1/4$ cup chopped pecans
2 tablespoons honey
1 cup Eggless Mayonnaise (page 46)
juice of 1 lemon

Blend the carrots, raisins, pineapple, pecans, and honey at high speed. Add the mayonnaise and the lemon juice until a coleslaw-like consistency is obtained. Chill and serve alone or on a bed of lettuce topped with sprouts.

SERVES 6.

Cauliflower Slaw

3 cups coarsely grated fresh cauliflower
1 cup chopped radishes
1/4 cup minced red onion
7 tablespoons Eggless Mayonnaise (page 46)
1 tablespoon fresh lemon juice
sprigs of parsley for garnish

In a bowl, mix together all the ingredients but the parsley. Garnish
with the sprigs of parsley.

SERVES 6.

SOUPS

Soup is something that people assume you just can't make without cooking. I thought so at first too. But as I got more proficient and creative in the kitchen, a whole new world opened up for me. Now soups, both hot and cold, are an essential part of my arsenal.

All soups should be made just prior to serving, that is if you want them hot (smile)! All of the soups are just as good cold, but they're still best if you make them right before you want to eat them.

MUSHROOM SOUP

1 cup plus 2 teaspoons tamari (or soy sauce)
1 tablespoon Italian seasoning
3 cups spring water, plus 1 cup very hot spring water
2 cups fresh mushrooms
1/2 avocado, pitted
1 teaspoon garlic powder

This is one of our favorites. When we first came up with it we couldn't believe it wasn't cooked. This is a good dish to serve to a "nonbeliever." Show your friends how good life as a raw vegetarian can be. The key is how you soak the mushrooms.

In a bowl, combine the cup of tamari, Italian seasoning, and 3 cups of water. Immerse the mushrooms in the tamari water and allow them to soak for at least 1 hour—but preferably overnight—in the refrigerator. The longer the better because the mushrooms become limp and meaty as they soak. Do not make the actual soup itself until you are ready to serve. When ready, combine in a blender: the cup of hot spring water (as for tea), tamari-marinated mushrooms (drained), the avocado, garlic powder, and the 2 teaspoons of tamari. Flick the blender from off to on and back to off as quickly as possible. This should create a thick, chunky, warm soup. If you desire fewer chunks, you may flick the blender on and off again. For no chunks (i.e., creamy soup), allow the blender to run for 15 to 20 seconds. Serve immediately.

SERVES 2.

POSEIDON'S SOUP

Poseidon is a delicious, quick, and easy soup to whip up if you happen to have made a meal including seaweed noodles and marinated veggies. This soup reminds me of oriental food.

¹/₄ cup Seaweed Noodles (page 35)
¹/₄ cup Marinated Veggies (page 33)
1–2 tablespoons tamari (or soy sauce—optional based on taste)
¹/₄ cup bean sprouts
1 teaspoon cayenne (optional)
1 cup hot spring water

Combine the seaweed noodles, marinated veggies, and tamari in a bowl. Next, add the sprouts and cayenne if desired (the cayenne can be very hot so be careful). Add the hot spring water last. Serve immediately.

SERVES 2.

BROCCOLI SOUP

1 cup broccoli florets
1 cup mushrooms
1 avocado, pitted and peeled
1 teaspoon tamari (or soy sauce)
1 cup hot spring water
1 teaspoon garlic powder

Combine all the ingredients in a food processor, and process until they're creamy. Serve immediately.

SERVES 2.

No more burning your tongue with soup bubbling over 100 degrees. All soup needs is a warm sensitive touch. In case you didn't know, broccoli comes in more ways than spears or florets. And it definitely doesn't have to come with cheese over it.

A standby. Something you can offer to your friends who are like: "Just give me something that I've heard of before!" It's delicious and easy to prepare.

VEGETABLE SOUP

2 cups Marinated Veggies (page 33)
$^1/_2$ cup Creamy Tahini Dressing (page 131)
1 teaspoon cayenne
1 cup hot spring water

Combine all the ingredients in a bowl, adding the hot spring water last. Mix well. Serve immediately.

SERVES 2.

CORN HUSKER SOUP

A soup can't get much more simple than this. If, of course, you've mastered the Corn Husker recipe.

2 cups Corn Husker (page 40)
1 cup hot spring water
1–2 tablespoons tamari (or soy sauce) or to taste

Blend all the ingredients in food processor until creamy.

SERVES 2.

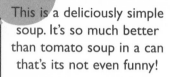

This is a deliciously simple soup. It's so much better than tomato soup in a can that's its not even funny!

Tomato 'n' Onion Soup

1 tomato, diced
1/4 onion, diced
1–2 tablespoons tamari (or soy sauce), as desired
1 teaspoon garlic powder
1 teaspoon chili powder
1 teaspoon chopped fresh cilantro
1 teaspoon chopped fresh parsley
1 teaspoon cayenne
1 1/2 cups hot spring water

In a bowl, combine all the ingredients except the water and stir together. Then add the hot spring water. (If you want to make a cream of tomato soup you can combine everything in the blender.) Serve immediately.

SERVES 2.

Mushroom-Broccoli-Avocado Soup

This is a very popular soup amongst patrons and staff of Delights of the Garden. In order to make it correctly you need to start about 24 hours before you wish to serve it. You first must soak the mushrooms in a solution of about 1 cup water and 1 tablespoon tamari.

5 mushrooms, presoaked as described above, drained
2 cups Broccoli Primavera (page 36)
$^1/_4$ onion
$^1/_2$–1 cup hot spring water
1–2 tablespoons tamari (or soy sauce), as desired
$^1/_4$ avocado, pitted and peeled
2 teaspoons chopped fresh cilantro
1 teaspoon cayenne

Combine all the ingredients in a blender or a food processor with the "S" blade installed. Quickly turn the blender on and then off, or use the pulse button on the food processor until the mixture is thick and chunky, but not homogenous.

SERVES 4.

Forget the piña colada, the pie, and the cake for now. Tease your taste buds with our coconut milk soup blended with spices.

COCONUT SOUP

¹/₂ cup coconut milk
¹/₂ cup corn, grated off the cob, or radishes, or kohlrabi, grated
¹/₄ cup rhubarb or cucumber juice (use a food processor)
1 tablespoon minced fresh chives or parsley
1 tablespoon honey or olive oil (optional)

In a bowl, beat together all the ingredients. Stir to mix and serve.

SERVES 1.

APPETIZERS

WEED WRAPS

FIRST MAKE THE WRAP BINDER:

juice of 1 lemon
1 tablespoon olive oil
1/2 teaspoon tamari (or soy sauce)

This is a delicious cousin to the Nori Rolls (a menu favorite, see next recipe). These are different because not only do they have a special kush inside but they are sealed with a solution you make called **wrap binder.** Sounds high-tech, doesn't it?

Mix the ingredients well until emulsified.

Now you're ready to make your rolls. You need:

2 cups soaked Kush (page 29)
1 tablespoon garlic powder
1 tablespoon onion powder
4 teaspoons curry powder
2 teaspoons chopped garlic
juice of 1/2 fresh orange
2 tablespoons sesame oil
1 tablespoon olive oil
1/4 cup tamari (or soy sauce)
1/2–1 teaspoon sea salt or salt substitute
6 nori seaweed sheets
3 leaves of green leaf lettuce
1 fresh tomato, halved and thinly sliced
1 cup peeled and thinly sliced cucumber
1 fresh beet, shredded

In a large bowl, mix the soaked kush, garlic, onion, and curry powders, and chopped garlic. Mix well until the dried seasonings are evenly distributed. To this mixture add the orange juice, oils,

and tamari. Mix well. If the mixture is not salty enough for your taste add sea salt or salt substitute. Next take a seaweed sheet and cover half of it evenly with the prepared kush. This should be followed by the lettuce cut or torn into nice-sized pieces to fit comfortably over the kush. The tomato slices should be layered over the lettuce followed by the cucumber slices. Last of all, the shredded beet should be evenly distributed in the center of all the vegetables.

Begin rolling the seaweed. The wrap must be very tight so that the contents will not fall out. Just before wrapping the final end, coat the edges of the seaweed with the wrap binder so that it will stay secured. You will then have a long wrap. Cut this into thirds. This is a wonderful meal that will truly tempt your taste buds.

MAKES 18 WEED WRAPS.

Nori Rolls

dried layer seaweed (nori seaweed), which comes in
8-inch square sheets
stuffing of your choice: Kush (page 29), Veggie Tuna (page 30), or
Nutmeat (page 31)
honey or maple syrup

Making nori rolls your first time may be a little tricky. Don't be frustrated if they keep falling apart on you. First, cut a sheet of seaweed into quarters (squares about 4 inches wide). Hold the seaweed open in your hand (with your hand cupped) and place a full tablespoon of the stuffing you are using in the center of the seaweed square. Roll the seaweed around the stuffing. Dip your finger in honey and run it across the inside edge of the seaweed. The honey should seal the roll. It is still best to place the rolls on a plate with the opening down so that gravity helps to keep it closed.

You can't get any veteran of Delights to eat a dish without some nori sheets on the side. They say you just can't taste it unless it's in a nori. We usually serve this appetizer with kush, veggie tuna, and nutmeat stuffed inside. Once you get the hang of it, though, you can take just about anything, roll it up, and let it melt in your mouth. Served on a bed of lettuce or sprouts, you can experiment with the arrangement. I always like to make a flower or a star, but who's to say you can't even build a house with them. Go for it!

STUFFED TOMATO

You can always dice it or slice it or use it to spice it, but who wants to see the same ol' boring tomato. Break away from the norm and stuff that sucker. With what, you say? Boy, have I got the perfect stocking stuffer this season . . . Spicy Kush (page 62)! When served as a side dish, we like to garnish it with some sprouts or a little parsley maybe. You anxious eaters might want to forget the good looks and get straight to the heart of the matter—the flavor . . . mmmmm!

First, cut out the area where the stem meets the tomato. Second, cut the tomato in half through the crown. Gouge out the insides of the tomato with a teaspoon and stuff the 2 halves of the tomato with spicy kush. Serve on a bed of alfalfa sprouts.

STUFFED PEPPER

With all the beautiful, bright colors these peppers come in, why on earth would you want to go and brown it up in some oil and a frying pan, or end up hiding it in the crevices of some other dish? You can get the great crispy taste of the bell pepper without going through all that. How? You guessed it. Stuff it! The best stuffer for this season is Nutmeat (page 31).

Use a red, green, or yellow bell pepper. Cut off the head of the pepper (so that it has a U shape). Stuff the pepper with nutmeat. You may serve the pepper on a bed of sprouts as a side dish, or build an entrée around it as a centerpiece.

I bet you're one of those who thinks avocado goes best stuffed in an avocado shell. Come on, use your imagination. Let's break out those stalks and avocado and take a dip or spread it on.

Avocado-Stuffed Celery

1 avocado, peeled and pitted
2 onion slices, finely chopped
1 sweet bell pepper, chopped
dried herbs of your choice, or vegetable seasoning
4 stalks celery, sliced into 4-inch lengths

In a bowl, mash the avocado. Combine with the onion, chopped pepper, and seasonings. Stuff the celery with the creamy mixture.

SERVES 2.

Nut-Stuffed Celery

2 tablespoons organic almond butter
1 tablespoon sunflower seeds, ground
1 teaspoon wheat germ
$1/8$ teaspoon sea salt
lemon juice (if needed for thinning)
4 stalks celery, sliced into 4-inch lengths

In a bowl, combine all the ingredients. Stuff the mixture into the pieces of celery.

SERVES 2.

Maybe you think the only thing you can eat celery with is peanut butter. Well that's not **the** only nut on earth. Don't be such a "nut case." Let's broaden those horizons with this special combination we've concocted just for you.

Scream of Mushrooms

1 pound mushrooms, cut into ⅛-inch-thick slices
1 small onion, chopped
¼ green bell pepper, finely chopped
1 garlic clove, chopped
juice of ½ lemon or orange
pinch of cayenne
½ teaspoon sea salt or salt substitute
2 tablespoons Eggless Mayonnaise (page 46)

In a bowl, mix all the ingredients together well and serve. This dish is excellent by itself, or as a dip, or on a bed of lettuce garnished with tomatoes, or served over seasoned kush.

SERVES 8.

Chips 'n' Dip

Convert the skeptics at your next get-together with this favorite of Delights of the Garden goers everywhere. Corn chips and nachos get out of the way. Who would've ever imagined dehydrated banana chips with a little cup of delicious uncooked Salsa (page 44) to dip them in would be so good?

If you're planning to make this, it's a good idea to start by making the salsa the day before so that the flavors can blend.

SAUCES

The sauces that you are going to prepare can go on a variety of our dishes. They are delicious—like icing on a cake. Whether you use the sauces for kush or as a dip for nori rolls— the wide range of flavors and varieties will enable you to have an endless list of combinations as well as various uses. The types range from essential elements of other dishes like barbeque sauce to radical ones like mango chutney. They all, however, have one secret that no canned or bottled sauce or dressing has— the love that you put into it.

Delights Natural Bar-Be-Que Sauce

Barbeque sauce is an essential ingredient in our Nutmeat recipe (page 31), Laron's Un-Chili (page 56), and various other dishes.

20 sun-dried tomatoes
4 tomatoes
1 cup honey, or 1¼ cups raisins
1 tablespoon vinegar (optional)
1 tablespoon molasses (optional)
2 tablespoons tamari (or soy sauce) or salt substitute
2 teaspoons dried thyme
2 teaspoons paprika
1 teaspoon chili powder

Soak the dried tomatoes for 2 hours in water. Combine all the ingredients (including the soaked tomatoes) in a food processor using the "S" blade, until a thick saucelike consistency is achieved.

Makes 3-4 cups.

This sauce is designed to accompany the Moussaka Marinara (page 59), but it's so good I could eat it out of a bowl all by itself like a soup. Don't be afraid to try it on kush and other things too.

MARINARA SAUCE

6 tomatoes
1 teaspoon dried sage (too much will ruin flavor)
2 tablespoons dried thyme
2 tablespoons chili powder
5 dried tomatoes
honey to taste
tamari (or soy sauce) to taste

Combine all the ingredients in a food processor. Process until smooth.

MAKES ABOUT 2 CUPS.

Sweet 'n' Sour Sauce

This recipe is primarily designed to be used in the Sweet and Sour Nutmeat recipe (page 31). You may also come up with some uses of your own for it. Hint: We've made kush using it.

¹/₃ cup dried pineapple chunks
Two ¹/₂ cups of spring water
2–3 tablespoons tamari (or soy sauce), as desired
1 tablespoon grated fresh ginger
¹/₂ cup lemon juice
1 tablespoon barbeque spice
2 teaspoons honey

Soak the pineapple in the first ¹/₂ cup of spring water until soft, about 10 minutes. Blend the pineapple and water in a food processor until the pineapple is smooth. Add tamari, ginger, lemon juice, and the second ¹/₂ cup of spring water. Continue to blend together. Next add the barbeque spice and honey. Continue blending. Taste and make any necessary adjustments.

MAKES ABOUT 1¹/₂ CUPS.

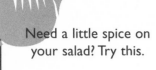

Need a little spice on your salad? Try this.

PEPPERY SAUCE

$1/2$ cup extra virgin olive oil
1 cup tamari (or soy sauce)
1 cup spring water
1 garlic clove, crushed
1 tablespoon chopped fresh parsley
1 teaspoon mixed herbs of your choice
2 teaspoons cayenne, or pinch of dried hot chili pepper
1 small onion, minced

In a bowl, mix the oil, tamari, water, and garlic. Stir well or blend together at high speed. Add the herbs and pepper slowly, blending all of the time. Last, add the onion. Store refrigerated in a bottle and shake well before using.

MAKES 3 CUPS.

MANGO CHUTNEY

flesh of 2 mangoes
2–3 pieces of gingerroot, peeled and minced
2 stalks celery, finely chopped
2 cups peeled and diced cucumbers
1 teaspoon lemon juice
2 tablespoons orange juice
pinch of tamari (or soy sauce) or salt substitute
1 tablespoon chopped fresh mint leaves
2 cups sweet red bell pepper
pinch of curry powder

Remove the peels and the stones from the mangoes. Chop mango flesh into bite-sized chunks. Stir together all the ingredients in a large bowl, and mix together. Serve on romaine lettuce or nori. This relish may also be used along with Avocado Grand (page 32).

MAKES ABOUT 5 CUPS.

Chutney is a pungent relish made of fruits, spices, and herbs. It can be used to garnish any number of dishes, from kush to fruit salad.

Bet you never thought you could make applesauce without cooking, but you can.

APPLESAUCE

5 ripe apples of your choice, preferably organically grown
1 cup unsweetened apple juice
1–2 tablespoons ground cinnamon or allspice, or to taste
1/4 cup honey to taste (optional)

Cut and core washed apples. If apples are nonorganic, peel them, as they will probably have a wax coating that washing will not remove. Quarter the apples and place in a blender, a few pieces at a time, with a small amount of apple juice, just enough to soften the apples while blending at high speed. Add cinnamon, allspice, or honey and refrigerate before serving.

MAKES 2 CUPS.

PEAR SAUCE

Try this variation of the applesauce concept.

5 ripe pears, preferably organically grown
2 very ripe bananas (optional)

Wash and quarter the pears. Place a few sections in the blender and liquefy. Add the remaining pieces slowly while blending. The bananas can be sliced and placed on top of each serving or blended into the mixture if you wish.

MAKES 2 CUPS.

A.K.A. "The Green Dressing"—this is the root of addiction for a good number of Delighters. I've had people come in the restaurant and ask for *cups* of this to take home with them. It's thick and memorably sweet.

SPINACH-TAHINI DRESSING

$^1/_2$ cup tahini
3 tablespoons tamari (or soy sauce)
handful of fresh spinach
2 cups spring water
1 cup raisins

Combine all the ingredients in a blender and blend for at least 1 minute, or until all the raisins are pulverized. This sauce is a favorite on kush, but works well on everything.

MAKES APPROXIMATELY $3^1/_2$ CUPS.

TOMATO-DILL DRESSING

One of our two special house dressings at the restaurant. Tomato-dill goes really well on almost anything, from a green salad to a plate of kush. It's creamy and "garlic-y."

$^3/_4$ cup tahini
3 tablespoons tamari (or soy sauce)
5 garlic cloves fresh
3 tomatoes
$^1/_2$ cup spring water
1 tablespoon chopped fresh dillweed

Combine all the ingredients in a blender and blend on high for several minutes. It is important to make sure that all garlic cloves have been pulverized. This sauce is best on kush, however, many people use it on everything.

MAKES APPROXIMATELY $3^1/_2$ CUPS.

A light summertime dressing that will work well with any green leafy salad. It was, however, specifically designed for the Spinach-Mushroom Salad (page 81).

Sunflower Dressing

2 tablespoons olive oil
1 tablespoon lemon juice
several pinches of dried tarragon
dash of grated nutmeg
4 cups torn fresh spinach leaves (optional)
lemon, for grated peel
2 tablespoons sunflower seeds

In a bowl, mix the oil, lemon juice, tarragon, and nutmeg. You may stop and use the dressing as is at this point, or you can blend the spinach leaves together with the other ingredients in a blender if you like. Grate a tiny bit of lemon peel onto the greens of your salad. Pour the dressing on your salad and toss with a fork. Sprinkle the sunflower seeds on top.

MAKES 1 CUP.

Tofu-Peanut Butter Dressing

This is a really thick and delicious dressing. Sweet and peanutty, it goes great on any green salad. People especially like it on the Waldorf Salad (page 71). A great combination (as anybody who's ever dipped apples in peanut butter knows)!

6 ounces tofu
3 tablespoons peanut butter
1 tablespoon lemon juice
touch of honey

Puree the ingredients in a blender.

MAKES APPROXIMATELY 1¹/₂ CUPS.

CREAMY SALAD DRESSING

This is what we call a classic. Easy to make and delicious—you know lazy people like me love this kind of thing.

Blend a few tomatoes on your blender's highest speed. Halve a ripe avocado, remove the pit and scoop out the creamy flesh into your blender. This recipe makes an excellent dressing but is also good as a dip for celery stalks, broccoli spears, and more!

MAKES APPROXIMATELY 1^1/$_2$ CUPS.

CREAMY TAHINI DRESSING

This dressing is a no-brainer. It's hard to fail with this formula. We used to hook this one up when we were too lazy to do anything else! But don't worry, it's scrumptious.

½ cup tahini
2 cups spring water
1 tablespoon fresh lemon juice
dash of tamari (or soy sauce)
cayenne (optional)

Place all the ingredients in a blender and blend until smooth and creamy. For thinner dressing, add more water.

MAKES 3 CUPS.

Here's a dressing for avocado lovers. So thick and creamy it's good enough to drink out of a cup!

Avocado Dressing

2 avocados, peeled and pitted, mashed
$1/2$ cup finely chopped onion
1 teaspoon kelp seasoning
1 teaspoon tamari (or soy sauce) or salt substitute
$1/4$ cup lemon juice

In a bowl, mix together all the ingredients, and enjoy this dressing on alfalfa sprouts or your favorite salad.

MAKES ABOUT 2 CUPS.

BALSAMIC VINAIGRETTE DRESSING

This is a delicious dressing that goes well with almost any green salad. It is also an essential part of some recipes (like the Cucumber and Tomato Delight, page 45). Don't cheat yourself by trying to use some kind of vinegar other than balsamic. It's more expensive, but worth it.

³/₄ cup balsamic vinegar
2 tablespoons tamari (or soy sauce)
1 ¹/₂ cups extra virgin cold-pressed olive oil
1 tablespoon Italian seasonings

Simply combine all ingredients in a bottle. Always shake the bottle before serving.

MAKES ABOUT 2 CUPS.

DESSERTS

Pie Shells

All of the following pie shells make enough for one 9-inch pie pan.

BATURI'S "PERFECT" PIE SHELL

2 cups unsweetened banana chips
1 cup dried pineapple
1 cup chopped pitted dates

In a food processor, process the banana chips until they are of a flourlike consistency. Add the dried pineapple and chopped dates. Process for about 2 to 3 minutes or until all of the ingredients begin to form a ball in the processor. At this point the shell is ready to be placed into a 9-inch pie pan. Press the dough out until it is evenly distributed in the pan. Edges may be fluted, if desired.

Osaze's Cream-Pie Shell

4 cups banana chips
1 cup dried pineapple

Using the "S" blade on your food processor, pulverize the mixture of the banana chips and pineapple. You should allow the processor to run for 8 to 10 minutes, or until the banana chips have no chunks at all! They should be powdery. Next, press the chips into a pie pan and refrigerate for 15 minutes.

Papa Grande Pie Shell

3 cups banana chips
$1/2$ cup dried pineapple
$1/2$ cup dried papaya
1 cup raisins

In a food processor using the "S" blade, combine all the ingredients. Allow the processor to run 2 to 3 minutes or until all of the ingredients are pulverized. The mixture should become one mass and begin to move in slow circles around the inside of the food processor. Remove the mixture and press it into a pie pan to an even thickness of $1/4$ to $3/8$ inch. You may now fill it with one of the fillings on the following pages or, as you become more experienced, make your own pie filling.

Sweet Potato Pie Shell

2 cups crushed almonds or pecans
I cup sunflower seeds
2 cups dates, soaked in spring water for 30 minutes

Using a food processor's "S" blade, blend all the above ingredients for 7 to 10 minutes, or until the dough is slightly sticky. Next, press the dough evenly into a 9-inch pie pan and fill the shell with the Sweet Potato Pie filling (page 143).

Fillings

Folks' first response when they try one of our pies is usually amazement that the pie doesn't contain any sugar. "How can it be so sweet? No sugar, well certainly it must be sweetened with honey." No! *None of the pies have any sugar or honey.* Good news for those of you who don't eat honey. Almost all of the pies rely purely on fruit for their sweetness. The sweet potato pie is sweetened with maple syrup. Use the shells from the previous section. Once you get the pie-making thing down, you can experiment with your own variations.

Each filling makes enough to fill the contents of one 9-inch pie pan.

This is a delicious pie that's a standard. It can be made basically all year round by substituting dried pineapple for fresh pineapple when fresh is unavailable.

TROPICAL FRUIT PIE

2 bananas, peeled
3 kiwis, peeled
1 1/2 pints fresh strawberries, washed and hulled
1/4 pineapple, peeled

Cut 1 banana, the kiwis, 1/2 pint of the strawberries, and the pineapple into small slices and line the bottom of a pie shell with the fruit slices laid flat. Next, combine the remaining strawberries and 1 banana in a food processor using the "S" blade. Process the fruit until pureed. Pour over the fruit in the shell.

Sweet Potato Pie

4 cups sweet potatoes, peeled and finely shredded
$1/2$ cup hot spring water
1 teaspoon pumpkin pie spice
2 teaspoons vanilla extract
2 teaspoons maple syrup
2 teaspoons lemon juice

In a food processor, blend all the ingredients until the mixture is smooth (about 5 minutes). You may want to stop after a couple of minutes and taste the filling, which should not have a gritty texture when tasted. If it does, continue processing. When done, spoon the filling into the pie shell and smooth out with a spatula. Cover with plastic wrap and refrigerate until ready to serve.

How in the world can you make a sweet potato pie without cooking? We silence the critics with this favorite of open-minded soul-food lovers. (Oh yeah, if you make it right it tastes just like yo' grandma's! People shouldn't necessarily be able to tell it's uncooked.) Note that in the pie shell section there's a special shell that is recommended for this pie.

Delights got started in Georgia—where peaches are king. So, you know we gotta make a peach pie. This one is a summertime favorite.

PASSIONATE PEACH PIE

6 medium ripe peaches, peeled and pitted
$1/2$ cup dried pineapple pieces
juice of 2 lemons
1 ripe kiwi, peeled
4 ripe strawberries, halved

Place 4 of the peaches into the food processor along with the pineapple pieces. Squeeze the juice of 1 lemon into the mixing bowl before processing. Process this mixture until the batter is of a smooth consistency. Pour batter into a prepared pie shell. Slice the remaining peaches into thin wedges and place them around the pie in a spiral. The kiwi should be peeled and thinly sliced and placed in the middle of the peach spirals along with the strawberry halves. Squeeze the remaining lemon juice on top of the pie to prevent discoloration.

Mango Madness Pie

If you get your hands on some ripe mangoes, you must make some Mango Madness Pie. The bright orange filling in a nice dark shell is worth taking pictures. So good it'll make ya' slap yo momma!

6 ripe mangos
$^1/_2$ cup chopped pitted dates
$^1/_4$ teaspoon ground cinnamon
$^1/_4$ teaspoon ground allspice
$^1/_4$ teaspoon grated nutmeg
$^1/_2$ cup sliced fruit of your choice for garnish

Peel 4 of the mangoes and slice the fruit away from the pits. Place the slices into the food processor along with the pitted dates and the spices. Process for about 2 minutes or until the mixture is of a smooth consistency. Peel the remaining mangoes and slice very neatly. The mangoes can be cut into strips and arranged alternately with other fruit garnishes of your choice.

The conservative Delighter is likely to try the tried-and-true apple pie. This pie can be made to taste surprisingly like actual cooked apple pie!

Apple Pie

5 medium-sized Golden Delicious apples
1 teaspoon apple pie spice
3 tablespoons lemon juice
1 cup dried pineapple pieces
1/4 cup banana chips as topping (optional)
1/4 cup raisins as topping (optional)
1/4 cup dried papaya as topping (optional)

Remove the skin and core from 4 of the apples. Cut these apples into chunks and place in a food processor with the "S" blade. Add the apple pie spice, lemon juice, and pineapple. Process until smooth. Take the remaining apple and cut into small pieces to be placed on the bottom of the pie. Once the mixture is smooth, pour over the chopped apple into the pie shell and top with crushed banana chips, raisins, and papaya.

Lemon Meringue Banana Cream Strawberry Cream

³/₄ cup honey
³/₄ cup lemon juice
3 bananas (for Banana Cream Pie)
2 cups strawberries, washed and hulled
(for Strawberry Cream Pie)
2 cups almonds or Brazil nuts

First, make 1¹/₂ cups of puree depending on the kind of pie
desired: for lemon meringue pie, combine the honey and lemon
juice in a blender or food processor. For banana cream pie, puree
the lemon juice, bananas, and honey. For strawberry cream pie,
puree the lemon juice, strawberries, and honey. Into a food
processor using the "S" blade, slowly pour the nuts. As the nuts are
being crushed, add the other ingredients and whip until creamy.
Fill the recommended pie shell (Osaze's Cream-Pie Shell, page
138). Allow to sit in the refrigerator for 15 minutes and serve.

"Old-School" has a unique Brazil nut shell. It's a simple but delicious pie. It's a throwback to the way we used to make all of our pies.

OLD-SCHOOL BANANA-RAISIN PIE

CRUST

10 ounces Brazil nuts
1 nutmeg (whole)
1 tablespoon vegetable oil

FILLING

4 ripe bananas
$1/2$ pound raisins
$1/4$ cup distilled water

Grind the nuts in a blender and pour into a pie pan. Grate the nutmeg and, along with the oil, add to the ground nuts. Mix together in a bowl to make the shell. Press this mixture to the bottom and sides of the pie pan. Next blend 3 of the bananas with all of the raisins. Add the water, a little at a time, using just enough to keep the mixture thick. Pour the mixture into the pie shell. Slice the remaining banana and decorate the top. Chill for at least 3 hours before serving.

VERY BERRY FRUIT PIE

¹/₂ cup dried pineapple pieces
¹/₂ cup fresh blackberries
¹/₂ cup fresh blueberries
¹/₂ cup fresh strawberries
¹/₂ cup mixed berries for garnish

In a food processor, combine all the ingredients except for the berries to be used for garnishing. Process for about 2 minutes or until the consistency of the mixture is smooth, then pour into the prepared pie shell. Garnish with the remaining berries.

This is a beautiful-looking pie. Its beauty comes from its rich purplish color and its texture. It sticks together better than a lot of cooked pies. The natural pectin in the blueberries makes the filling gel so well.

BOOMING BLACKBERRY PIE

1 ½ pints fresh blackberries
¾ cup blueberries
½ cup dried pineapple pieces
5 fresh strawberries, sliced

Wash the berries and remove the stems. In the food processor, place 1 pint of the blackberries and all of the blueberries along with the dried pineapple. (Blueberries will help the pie congeal because of their natural pectin.) Blend well and pour into a 9-inch pie shell. Top with the strawberries.

BATURI'S BLUEBERRY PIE

1½ pints fresh blueberries
½ cup dried pineapple pieces
3–4 attractive strawberries for garnish
1 ripe kiwi, sliced

Wash the berries and remove any stems or leaves. In a food processor, add 1 pint of the berries and the dried pineapple. Process for about 2 minutes or until the mixture is smooth. Do not process too long. Blueberries have natural pectin and will congeal in the processor. Pour the mixture into the prepared pie shell and decorate with the remaining berries and other fruits.

SCRUMPTIOUS STRAWBERRY- BLUEBERRY PIE

$^1\!/_2$ pint fresh blueberries
$^1\!/_2$ pint fresh strawberries
$^1\!/_2$ cup dried pineapple pieces
fruits of your choice for garnish

Wash the berries and remove the stems. Put into a food processor along with the dried pineapple and blend until the mixture is smooth. Pour into a 9-inch prepared pie shell, and decorate with fruits of your choice.

Banana Cake:
The Ever-Flavorful
"Eduardo"

The new smash hit of the Georgetown Delights. It's an uncooked banana cake that you'll never forget.

Shell:

2 cups banana chips
1 cup raisins
2 bananas, sliced

Pulverize the banana chips and raisins in a food processor using the "S" blade. Spoon this into the bottom of an 8-inch square cake pan. Only apply to the bottom of the pan. Next add a layer of fresh banana slices.

Cake Filling:

3 cups banana chips, plus extra for topping
1 cup almonds
4 cups dates and raisins, soaked for at least 30 minutes in spring water
2 whole bananas
3 cups almond milk (see page 46) or creamy soy milk
1 cup dried pineapple pieces
1 teaspoon ground cinnamon
2 teaspoons vanilla extract

Combine the 3 cups banana chips and the almonds in a food processor or blender. Blend for about 3 to 4 minutes or until they reach a flourlike consistency. Next, combine the soaked dates and raisins, bananas, and almond or soy milk. Add all the remaining ingredients. Spoon the filling into the pan. Finally top it off with crumbled banana chips. Refrigerate until set.

DOWN AND DIRTY BROWNIES

It ain't no joke! . . .
Introducing the world's
only uncooked brownie.

3 cups banana chips
1/2 cup dried pineapple pieces
1/2 cup dried papaya pieces
1 1/2 cups raisins
1/3 cup honey (optional)
1/3 cup carob powder

Combine the banana, pineapple, papaya, raisins, and honey (optional) in a food processor using the "S" blade. Process until the banana chips are thoroughly pulverized. The mixture should be a very sticky blob. Now place the mixture in a large mixing bowl that has been lined with the carob powder. Knead the carob powder into the mixture. Finally, compress the mixture into a 12- × 18-inch brownie baking pan.

You may stop here, or you may want to coat the brownie with a carob glaze as follows: Combine 3 tablespoons honey with 1/4 cup carob powder. Slowly add hot water to the mixture, stirring as you go. The hot water should dissolve the honey and there should be no clumps of carob in the mix. Add no more than 1/4 cup hot water. After glazing the brownies, you may want to sprinkle some coconut on top and/or some ground almonds.

Now you're done. Cover with plastic wrap. Allow to sit for at least an hour. Brownies don't need to be refrigerated!

MAKES ABOUT 30.

Make these delicious treats and find out why we can never keep them in stock at the restaurants.

UN-COOKIES

3 cups banana chips
1/2 cup dried pineapple pieces
1/2 cup dried papaya
1 cup raisins
1 pound raw peanut butter

Combine all the ingredients except the peanut butter in a food processor with the "S" blade installed. Let run for about a minute. In a large mixing bowl, cut the peanut butter into the dried fruit mixture. Knead the mixture thoroughly. Using your hands, shape the batter into 1/2-inch-thick cookies about 3 inches in diameter. Place the un-cookie in a dehydrator and allow them to dehydrate for as long as necessary to become firm. This will take several hours since the temperature of a dehydrator should never exceed 120 degrees Fahrenheit.

MAKES ABOUT TWO DOZEN UN-COOKIES DEPENDING ON
HOW LARGE YOU MAKE THEM.

MUFFINS

3 cups banana chips
1 cup dried pineapple pieces
1/2 cup fresh fruit of your choice

Blend all the ingredients in a food processor until moist. Using your hands, compress the mixture into a muffin pan, and neatly mold into muffin shapes. Serve immediately.

MAKES 6-8 MUFFINS.

If you've ever been to one of our Sunday brunches, you may remember the muffins. They're delicious and simple to prepare in the food processor. You get to choose what kind of muffins you're going to make by selecting the fruit to use in the recipe. Try blueberry or strawberry. Throw in fresh bananas for the fruit and some nuts to make a "banana-nut" muffin.

FRUITCAKE

A fruitcake that your friends will actually eat! It has a taste resembling fruitcake but in reality is much better. Of course, no wrapping it in a rum-soaked cloth either.

1 cup dates
1 cup raisins
1 cup wheat germ
1 cup mixed dried fruits
1 cup chopped nuts
1 cup orange juice
$^1\!/_2$ cup clover honey

Cut the dates into small pieces. Soak the dates and raisins in warm spring water overnight. Drain. Combine all the ingredients in a large bowl. Pack firmly into a waxed paper–lined loaf pan. Place a weight on top and set in the refrigerator for 1 or 2 days. Slice and serve.

MAKES 10 SERVINGS.

FRUITY NUT CREAM

It's kind of reminiscent of ice milk. Like ice cream but lighter and in this case, *fruitier.*

1 cup almonds
1 cup apple juice
2 cups fruit (strawberries, peaches, or any other)
1 banana
2 tablespoons safflower oil

Blend all the ingredients together in an electric blender. Pour into a container and put in the freezer for 1 to 2 hours. Do not let freeze solid.

MAKES 4 SERVINGS.

We used to call these "fruit nut balls." You can make Afrikande into little balls and roll them in some coconut.

AFRIKANDE

1 cup dates
1 cup raisins
$^1/_4$ cup coconut flakes, plus additional for coating
1 cup nuts of your choice (almonds, pecans, or Brazil nuts), plus additional for coating

Combine all the ingredients in a food processor and process to a paste-like consistency. Shape into balls or shape into a square and cut into small bite-sized squares. Coat with grated coconut and sprinkle nuts on top. Refrigerate.

MAKES ABOUT 15 BALLS.

Marietta Street Ice Cream

Immortalized as the cornerstone of the first summer of Delights of the Garden. It had people flocking to 136 Marietta Street. It's so simple . . . but so good!

3 bunches of extremely ripe bananas

Peel the bananas, place them in plastic bags or containers and freeze them. When ready to eat, remove the bananas and put them into a continuous feed juicer (i.e., Champion brand) with a block on the pulp discharge. The product will be cold, smooth, and sweet. It will resemble soft ice cream in taste and consistency. Various flavors can be made by first freezing fruit (strawberries, blueberries, kiwi, dates) and then putting them into the juicer intermittently with the bananas. You can also try peanut butter ice cream, by putting about 2 tablespoons raw peanut butter in the juicer with the bananas.

MAKES 1 SERVING.

If Marietta Street Ice Cream (see preceding recipe) is the soft ice cream, then this is the "hard" ice cream. Just like ice cream, you need to churn this periodically, and therefore it takes more time to make.

BANANA ICE CREAM

12 very ripe bananas
1 cup maple syrup or honey
2 cups orange juice
$1/2$ cup chopped nuts (almonds work well)

Place a third of each of the following ingredients into a blender: the bananas, syrup or honey, and orange juice. Blend until smooth. Transfer the mixture to a bowl and blend with another third of the bananas, syrup or honey, and juice. Then blend the last third. Combine and stir in the nuts. Place the mixture in a shallow freezer tray and freeze overnight. The texture is improved by stirring at intervals.

MAKES ABOUT 8 SERVINGS.

POPS-I-FRUITY

any fresh seasonal fruit (peaches, strawberries, mangoes)

Blend at high speed. Put the liquid in an ice cube tray or in small cups. When partially frozen, insert toothpicks. Allow to freeze completely.

Didn't your mom used to make those frozen juice Popsicles in the freezer for you in the summertime. Well, here's their second coming!

DRINKS

Trying to cool off on a hot summer day? Or running late for work in the morning and don't have time to eat breakfast? Need a little boost for your workout? These drinks are made for you. All very simple and quick to make. But delicious and nutritious—useful for lots of different occasions.

GINGER BEER

4 ginger roots, grated
3 sticks cinnamon, broken in half
1 teaspoon cloves
$1/2$ cup freshly squeezed lemon juice
honey to taste

Put the ginger and spices in a 1-gallon glass or ceramic bottle and fill with hot water. (Don't use a plastic container unless you want the ginger beer to taste like plastic.) Put the loosely capped bottle in a paper bag and let it sit for 4 days. That's right, 4 days! Strain, add the lemon juice and honey to taste. Serve on the rocks (that means with ice, slick).

MAKES ABOUT 1 GALLON.

Bring Jamaica to your kitchen with our twist on this Caribbean classic. Now enjoy it without carbonation and without the damaging effects of cooking. But don't expect to drink it tonight. As you'll soon see, it's going to take a little while to make it! It's well worth the wait.

Want to get the most out of your food? . . . Juice it. You can conquer a whole bag of carrots in 1 cup of carrot juice. If you haven't already experienced the fun of juicing experimentation, our veggie drink will definitely hook you. Fresh veggies are the best, quickest source of lots of vitamins and minerals (see "Vitamin and Mineral Index"). And when they are freshly juiced, the taste is incredible.

VEGGIE DRINK

2 tomatoes
1 sweet bell pepper
1 cucumber
3 sprigs of parsley
2 carrots
1 stalk celery
1/2 teaspoon kelp powder, or to taste

Juice the veggies and season to taste. You can even try a dash of cayenne pepper in it!

MAKES 1 SERVING.

WAKE-UP SHAKE-UP

BLEND AT LOW SPEED:

1 cup fresh orange juice
1 ripe banana

Do whatever it takes. Search high and low, but make sure you get the ripest bananas and juiciest oranges!

MAKES 1 CUP.

Throw away that coffeepot and dig out that blender. This recipe is a surprisingly simple, yet delicious way to start your day. If you've never had bananas and oranges together you'll never want to have them any other way again.

Fruit Smoothie

Use any very fresh, ripe seasonal fruit: bananas, mangoes, strawberries, peaches, etc. To sweeten, add dates or raisins. Blend in a blender at high speed and add distilled water a little at a time until the desired consistency is obtained. A tip: if you keep all of the ingredients in the refrigerator beforehand, the drink will automatically be cool when you make it.

Banana-Date Shake

1 cup fresh fruit juice (apple, pear, or grape)
two bananas
3 dates
spring water

Peel and freeze the bananas in a plastic bag. Pit the dates (about 2 large or 4 small per serving). Make the juice in an electric juicer or on the highest speed of a blender with a little spring water. To the juice, add the frozen bananas, and blend at high speed until smooth.

SERVES 1.

This "shake" is somewhere between soft ice cream and a milkshake. You can control the consistency by how much water you use in the recipe.

This is the real thing here. If you don't cut corners, but actually get a real coconut and juice the pineapples yourself, you will be in for a real treat. Not to mention that it will *really* fill you up.

Piña Colada

2 ripe bananas
2 cups pineapple juice
water from a whole coconut
honey to taste
crushed ice
sprig of mint

Liquefy all the ingredients except garnish in a blender. Garnish with the sprig of mint.

Serves 1.

Date Shake

5 apples
1 ripe banana
3–6 soft pitted dates

Juice the apples to make 1 cup of apple juice. Place in a blender and add the fresh banana and dates. Blend at a high speed until creamy. May be made thicker with more bananas or thinner with more apple juice or spring water.

MAKES 1 SERVING.

Are you ready for a treat? This time you get to use both the blender and the juicer. The best of both worlds.

FOOD NUTRIENT INDEX

In making dietary changes it's important to know what is what exactly. This Food Nutrient Index section gives detailed listings of the protein, fat, and carbohydrate contents of the food types that *Delights of the Garden* advocates. The Vitamin and Mineral Index which follows discusses every major vitamin and mineral in terms of its definition, function, uses, sources, and depletors.

Percentage of Calories from Protein, Fat, and Carbohydrates

Fruits

	Protein	Fat	Carbo.
Apples	1	8	91
Apricots	7	4	89
Avocados	5	81	14
Bananas	5	3	92
Blackberries	7	13	80
Blueberries	5	7	80
Cantaloupes	8	3	89
Cherimoyas	5	4	91
Cherries	8	4	88
Cranberries	3	13	84
Custard apples	7	5	88
Dates	3	0	97

Figs	6	5	89
Gooseberries	8	5	87
Grapefruit	5	2	93
Grapes	8	13	79
Honeydew melons	10	8	82
Lemons	13	7	80
Loganberries	6	8	86
Mangoes	4	5	91
Olives	5	91	4
Oranges	8	4	88
Papayas	6	2	92
Peaches	6	2	92
Pears	5	6	89
Persimmons	3	3	94
Pineapples	3	3	94
Plums	3	0	97
Pomegranates	3	5	92
Prunes	4	1	95
Raisins	3	0	97
Raspberries	8	16	76
Strawberries	8	12	80
Tangerines	7	4	89
Watermelons	8	7	85

Vegetables

	Protein	Fat	Carbo.
Artichokes	22	3	75
Asparagus	32	6	62
Bamboo shoots	31	8	61
Beet greens	30	9	61
Beets	14	2	84
Broccoli	36	6	58
Brussels sprouts	36	6	58

	Protein	Fat	Carbo.
Cabbage	18	7	75
Carrots	10	4	86
Cauliflower	34	6	60
Celery	17	6	77
Chinese cabbage	28	6	66
Chives	34	0	66
Collards	34	12	54
Corn, sweet	11	7	82
Cucumbers	20	7	73
Dandelion greens	20	13	67
Eggplant	18	9	73
Endive	29	5	66
Garlic	20	0	80
Kale	40	11	49
Lettuce	29	12	59
Mustard greens	31	13	56
New Zealand spinach	37	12	51
Okra	22	8	70
Onions	15	3	82
Parsley	30	12	58
Parsnips	9	6	85
Peas, green	30	4	66
Peppers, green bell	20	8	72
Peppers, hot chile	14	4	86
Potatoes	1	1	88
Pumpkin	12	8	80
Radishes	10	1	89
Shallots	16	0	84
Spinach	40	9	51
Squash, summer	20	5	75
Sweet potatoes	6	3	91
Tomatoes	17	8	75
Turnip greens	35	8	57

	Protein	Fat	Carbo.
Turnips	13	7	75
Watercress	40	11	49
Yams	8	2	90
Zucchini	26	6	78

Grains

	Protein	Fat	Carbo.
Barley	9	3	88
Buckwheat, dark	13	7	88
Corn flour	9	6	85
Oatmeal	15	16	69
Rice, brown	15	16	69
Rice, polished	7	1	92
Rye flour, dark	18	7	75
Rye flour, light	11	2	87
Spaghetti, white	14	3	83
Wheat flour, white	12	3	85
Wheat flour, whole	16	5	79
Wheat germ	29	25	46
Wild rice	16	2	82

Legumes

	Protein	Fat	Carbo.
Broad beans	31	3	66
Cowpeas	28	6	66
Garbanzo beans	23	12	65
Kidney beans	26	4	70
Lentils	29	3	68
Lima beans	25	4	71
Mung beans	28	3	69
Mung bean sprouts	34	5	61

	Protein	Fat	Carbo.
Snap beans, green	21	6	73
Soybean curd, tofu	40	48	12
Soybean flour, full fat	33	40	27
Soybeans	32	37	31
Soybean sprouts	43	20	37
Soy sauce	31	17	52
Split peas	28	3	69
White beans	26	4	70

Nuts and Seeds

	Protein	Fat	Carbo.
Almonds	11	77	12
Cashew nuts	12	68	20
Chestnuts	6	7	87
Coconut	4	85	11
Filberts, hazelnuts	8	81	11
Lychees	6	5	89
Peanuts	18	68	14
Pine nuts	8	80	12
Pistachios	13	74	13
Pumpkin seeds	20	70	10
Sesame seeds	13	75	12
Sunflower seeds	17	69	14
Walnuts, black	13	79	8

Note: Data derived from "Nutritive Value of American Foods in Common Units," *Agriculture Handbook* No. 456.

VITAMIN AND MINERAL INDEX

VITAMINS

Vitamin A

Principal Sources: Carrots, green and yellow vegetables, fruits, dried apricots, sweet potatoes, sweet red bell peppers, dried peaches. Herbs: alfalfa, blessed thistle, capsicum, fenugreek, passionflower, parsley, slippery elm, ginseng, skullcap, papaya, saw palmetto, rose hips, red raspberry, uva-ursi, peppermint, eyebright, dandelion, damiana, catnip, chaparral.

Function: This vitamin assists the body's immune system and helps protect against the harmful effects of radiation and air pollution. It will help prevent the development of kidney stones and reduces night blindness. In addition, vitamin A aids with the secretion of gastric juices for protein digestion, builds bones and teeth, prolongs longevity and delays senility, maintains and repairs healthy tissue.

Therapeutic Uses: Acne, alcoholism, allergies, athlete's foot, arthritis, asthma, bronchitis, hay fever, colds, diabetes, eczema, heart

disease, hepatitis, migraine, psoriasis, sinusitis, stress, tooth and gum diseases.

Vitamin A Depletors: Contraceptives, cortisone, prednisone, alcohol, estrogen, mineral oil, most drugs, coffee, air pollutants, interior lighting.

Vitamin B (Thiamine)

Water soluble—small amounts stored in heart, liver, and brain.

Principle Sources: Wheat germ, sunflower seeds, peanuts with skin, sesame seeds, pinto and white beans, dried peas, millet. Herbs: barberry, burdock, kelp, dulse, gotu kola, alfalfa, ginseng, skullcap, papaya, peppermint, spirulina, slippery elm, sage, parsley, butcher's-broom, feverfew.

Function: Thiamine is essential for the health of the entire nervous system and for the proper functioning of the digestive system. It helps the body to utilize energy from carbohydrate foods and is needed during pregnancy, lactation, and strenuous exercise. Thiamine also nourishes the brain, eye, ears, hair, heart, liver, kidneys. This vitamin helps prevent excessive fatty deposits on the wall of arteries, aids the treatment of herpes, repels biting insects, and protects against effects of lead.

Therapeutic Uses: Alcoholism, anemia, depression, irritability, congestive heart failure, constipation, diarrhea, diabetes, nausea, indigestion, mental illness, stress, rapid heart rate, seasickness, air sickness, beriberi, shingles.

Vitamin B Depletors: Negative emotions, alcohol, cooking heat, caffeine, excess sugar, stress, tobacco, surgery, raw fish and shellfish, muscle relaxants, and sulfa drugs.

Vitamin B₂ (Riboflavin)

Water soluble—small amounts stored in skeletal muscles.

Principal Sources: Dry hot red peppers, almonds, wheat germ, wild rice, mushrooms, turnip greens, safflower seeds, millet, dried peas, white beans, parsley, kale, cashews, sesame seeds. Herbs: alfalfa, barberry, gotu kola, spirulina, parsley, kelp, hops, ginseng, slippery elm, sarsaparilla, papaya, and peppermint.

Function: Vitamin B_2 is necessary for proper enzyme formation; normal growth; tissue formation; and the metabolism of fats, carbohydrates, and protein. It helps maintain good vision, skin, nails, and hair. Also, it assists the body in the formation of antibodies and in the production of red blood cells and hormones. B_2 is good for pregnant women as it helps with the absorption of iron and provides extra stamina during periods of lactation.

Therapeutic Uses: Arteriosclerosis, baldness, cystitis, hypoglycemia, mental retardation, muscular diseases, nervous disorders, nausea in pregnancy, obesity, stress, dizziness, trembling, depression, and hysteria.

Vitamin B_2 Depletors: Alcohol, birth control pills, coffee, radiation, tobacco, ultraviolet light, drugs, estrogen, and sugar.

Vitamin B₃ (Niacinamide)

Water soluble—stored in liver.

Principal Sources: Rice and wheat bran, peanuts with skin, hot red peppers, dry wild rue, sesame seeds, sunflower seeds, brown rice, wheat and barley, green vegetables, beans. Herbs: butcher's-broom, kelp, horsetail, hops, gotu kola, feverfew, spirulina, slippery elm, ginseng, sarsaparilla, red raspberry, red clover, peppermint, parsley, papaya, eyebright, damiana, barberry.

Function: Vitamin B_3 participates in the conversion of the amino acid tryptophan into niacin. B_3 helps promote good physical and mental health. It is good for preventing high cholesterol, high blood pressure, and heart attacks. B_3 is also essential for the production of male and female sex hormones, helps regulate blood sugar level in hypoglycemia, and eases attacks of diarrhea.

Therapeutic Uses: Acne, baldness, diarrhea, halitosis, high blood pressure, leg cramps, migraine, night blindness, hypertension, tooth decay, poor circulation, stress, backaches, poor memory, senility, and schizophrenia.

Vitamin B_3 Depletors: Caffeine, antibiotics, alcohol, sleeping pills, estrogen, excessive sugar, refined carbohydrates, sulfa drugs.

Vitamin B_5 (Pantothenic Acid)

Water soluble.

Principal Sources: Queen bee royal jelly, brewer's yeast, molasses, soybeans, peanuts, wheat germ, dried peas and beans, whole grains. Herbs: barberry, parsley, kelp, hops, gotu kola, papaya, peppermint, ginseng, slippery elm, spirulina.

Function: Pantothenic acid is necessary for the proper functioning of the adrenal glands and hormones and is needed for proper digestion; metabolization of fats, carbohydrates, and protein; antibody formation; and regulation of growth stimulation.

Therapeutic Uses: Helps with hypoglycemia, allergies, anemia, arthritis, asthma, diarrhea, eczema, muscle cramps, loss of hair, premature aging, respiratory infection, Addison's disease, baldness, cystitis, diabetes, depression, alcoholism, tooth decay, wound healing.

Vitamin B_5 Depletors: Methyl bromide, insecticidal fumigant, alcohol, coffee, heat in cooking, sulfa drugs, estrogen, and sleeping pills.

Vitamin B_6
(Pyridoxine Hydrochloride)

Water soluble.

Principal Sources: Brewer's yeast, wheat germ, blackstrap molasses, honey, almonds, soybeans, carrots, kale, okra, spinach. Herbs: alfalfa, slippery elm, ginseng, spirulina, sarsaparilla, peppermint, papaya, parsley, kelp, hops, gotu kola, feverfew.

Function: Vitamin B_6 is used for conversion of the protein foods into amino acids. It is involved in the production of antibodies and helps to maintain a balance of potassium and sodium for the entire nervous system. It may prevent the formation of kidney stones and is thought to convert oxalic acid into a harmless form. B_6 also protects the body from the harmful effects of gamma radiation and Xrays. Without B_6 the body can barely tolerate glucose and becomes sensitive to insulin.

Therapeutic Uses: Headaches, anemia, hypoglycemia, epilepsy, insomnia, arthritis, asthma, arteriosclerosis, Parkinson's disease, cataracts, weight control, high cholesterol levels, eczema, convulsions, heart attacks.

Vitamin B_6 Depletors: Alcohol, oral contraceptives cause severe loss, canning and roasting, estrogen, long storage, most drugs, and stress.

Vitamin B_9 (Folic Acid)

Water soluble—small amounts stored in liver.

Principal Sources: Green leafy vegetables, fresh mushrooms,

sprouts, liver, kidneys, brewer's yeast, wheat germ, soybeans. Herbs: barberry, ginseng, feverfew, kelp, hops, gotu kola, parsley, peppermint, papaya, slippery elm, spirulina.

Function: Folic acid stimulates the production of hydrochloric acid and is essential for the absorption of iron and calcium. Along with vitamin B_{12} and C the body uses this vitamin to break down protein foods, form new red blood cells, produce antibodies, and maintain sex organs.

Therapeutic Uses: Alcoholism, anemia, arteriosclerosis, baldness, intestinal parasites, diarrhea, dropsy, menstrual problems, mental illness, fatigue, stomach and leg ulcers, stress, blood disorders.

Vitamin B_9 Depletors: Contraceptives, high temperatures, alcohol, coffee, stress, sulfa drugs, tobacco, estrogen, food processing, barbiturates, Dilantin.

Vitamin B_{12} (Cobalamin)

Slightly water soluble.

Principal Sources: Soybeans, wheat germ, brewer's yeast, almonds, carrots. Herbs: alfalfa, ginseng, bee pollen, dandelion, spirulina.

Function: Calcium is needed for the proper assimilation of this nutrient. It is the only vitamin which contains a mineral element—cobalt. Cobalamin is used to metabolize carbohydrates, fats, and proteins. B_{12} is necessary for the body's use of amino acids and vitamin D and the absorption of iron.

Therapeutic Uses: Fatigue, nervous irritability, poor memory, allergies, alcoholism, pernicious anemia, ulcers, bronchial asthma, angina pectoris, bursitis, epilepsy, diabetes, hypoglycemia, insomnia, obesity, shingles, stress, neuritis, mental illness, osteoporosis, hepatitis, multiple sclerosis. As much as 1,000 micrograms found to be effective in treating pernicious anemia with no ill effects.

Vitamin B_{12} Depletors: Laxatives, alcohol, antibiotics, aspirin, diuretics, antacids, tobacco, caffeine, estrogen, sleeping pills, contraceptives, intestinal parasites, cooking.

Vitamin B_{13} (Orotic Acid)

Principal Sources: Found in root vegetables and fruit.

Function: B_{13} aids the body in using folic acid and vitamin B_{12}.

Therapeutic Uses: For health of nervous system, efficient brain functioning, and multiple efficiency. Deficiency may lead to liver disorders, cell degeneration, and premature aging.

Vitamin B_{13} Depletors: Water and sunlight.

Vitamin B_{15}

Water soluble.

Principal Sources: Brewer's yeast, sesame seeds, whole brown rice, pumpkin seeds, apricot kernels, grains.

Function: Vitamin B_{15} improves blood circulation and the body's ability to use oxygen. This nutrient also assists in the metabolism of protein, fat, and sugar. It may help to prevent premature aging as well as serving as a detoxifying agent that protects against possible cancer-causing chemicals and pollutants.

Therapeutic Uses: High blood pressure, high cholesterol levels, rheumatism, angina, asthma, hypertension, emphysema, alcoholism, cancer, hepatitis, cirrhosis of the liver, arteriosclerosis, and headaches.

Vitamin B_{15} Depletors: Alcohol, coffee, sunlight, most laxatives, and water.

Vitamin B$_{17}$ (Laetrile)

Principal Sources: Almonds, apricot kernels, cherries, nectarines, peaches, plums, peas, broad beans, apples, papayas, alfalfa seeds, berries, sorghum, millet, buckwheat, alfalfa leaves.

Function: This contains natural cyanide used to kill cancer cells. It is believed by some to have cancer-controlling and -preventing properties that literally poison the malignant cell while nourishing all the other cells. Vitamin B$_{17}$ also stimulates the hemoglobin or red blood cell count.

Therapeutic Uses: Cancer, sickle-cell anemia. Excessive amounts can be dangerous.

Vitamin B$_{17}$ Depletors: Alcohol, coffee.

PABA (Para-Aminobenzoic Acid)

Water soluble—stored in body tissue.

Principal Sources: Brewer's yeast, wheat germ. Herbs: papaya.

Function: PABA is necessary for the process of synthesizing folic acid, the formation of blood cells, and protein metabolism. It also enhances the intestinal flora activity.

Therapeutic Uses: Eczema, parasites, nervousness, baldness, constipation, overactive thyroid, rheumatic fever, stress, infertility. Continual high doses (over 30 milligrams) can be toxic and cause depression.

PABA Depletors: Coffee, sulfa drugs, alcohol, estrogen, food processing, water.

Choline

Water soluble.

Principal Sources: Peas, peanuts, brewer's yeast, wheat germ, lecithin, sesame seeds, turnip greens, string beans, spinach. Herbs: barberry.

Function: Choline maintains healthy liver, kidneys, brain, and heart while strengthening weak capillaries. It regulates cholesterol levels; assists in preventing gallstones and in the digestion of all types of fatty foods; needed for storage of minerals, especially calcium, and vitamin A. In addition, this vitamin promotes even distribution of fats around the body and combines with other ingredients in the liver to produce lecithin.

Therapeutic Uses: High cholesterol levels, hepatitis, arteriosclerosis, baldness, constipation, hypoglycemia, dizziness, multiple sclerosis, glaucoma, asthma, eczema, alcoholism, muscular dystrophy, heart trouble, high blood pressure, hardening of the arteries.

Choline Depletors: Water, sulfa drugs, estrogen, food processing, alcohol, excessive sugar.

Inositol

Water soluble.

Principal Sources: Soybean, lecithin, molasses, cantaloupes, lima beans, oranges, wheat germ, sesame seeds, whole wheat bread, brewer's yeast.

Function: Inositol cleanses the blood of excessive fats, which helps the heart muscles and reduces blood cholesterol levels by producing lecithin. It stimulates digestive action, promotes hair growth, stimulates normal growth and survival of cells in bone marrow and eye membranes.

Therapeutic Uses: Baldness, constipation, eczema, heart disease, hardening of the arteries, arteriosclerosis, cirrhosis of the liver, glaucoma, obesity, gall bladder trouble.

Inositol Depletors: Caffeine, insect sprays, alcohol, sulfa drugs, water.

Vitamin C (Ascorbic Acid)

Water soluble—small amount stored in adrenal cortex.

Principal Sources: Acerola cherry juice, raw hot red peppers, as well as sweet red and green bell peppers, oranges, tomatoes. Herbs: catnip, ginseng, hops, hawthorne berries, eyebright, rose hips, parsley, passionflower, juniper berries, lobelia, aloe vera, burdock, dandelion, horsetail, bayberry.

Function: Ascorbic acid helps prevent infection by increasing and speeding up the activity of white blood cells that destroy bacteria. It plays a primary role in the formation of collagen and is essential for good teeth and bones. Vitamin C is good for proper glandular activity, especially the adrenal glands. It helps eliminate cancer-causing substances by reinforcing the defense system. Cholesterol is converted into bile salts by vitamin C for the prevention of gallstones and kidney stones. It aids in the absorption of iron and enables the storage of folic acid. In nature, vitamin C is always in combination with bioflavinoids. This nutrient is more effective when taken in frequent small doses. Finally, vitamin C is used by the body in several other ways, including iodine conservation, antioxidant activities, detoxification of drugs, protection against nitrates and nitrites.

Therapeutic Uses: Arthritis, colds, alcoholism, allergies, tonsillitis, ear infections, atherosclerosis, baldness, carbon monoxide poisoning, heavy metal poisoning, cystitis, drug addiction, hypoglycemia, heart disease, hepatitis, obesity, prickly heat, sinusitis, tooth decay, stress, asthma, radiation.

Vitamin C Depletors: Alcohol, air pollution, cigarette smoking, birth control pills, antibiotics, stress, aspirin, pain-killers, diuretics, cortisone.

Vitamin D

Fat soluble—stored in skin, brain, liver, bones.

Principal Sources: Spinach. Herbs: fenugreek, eyebright, alfalfa.

Function: Vitamin D is essential for the proper functioning of the glandular and nervous system. Its main function is to regulate all mineral and vitamin metabolism, especially calcium, phosphorus, and vitamin A. It is produced naturally by the action of sunlight with an oily substance, ergosterol. With vitamins A and C, this nutrient helps to prevent colds.

Therapeutic Uses: Acne, alcoholism, rickets, colds, eye infection, tooth decay, myopia, conjunctivitis, rheumatoid arthritis, allergies, cystitis, psoriasis, stress, cramps, constipation. Toxicity—25,000 I.U. over an extended period of time. Synthetic vitamin D more toxic than natural.

Vitamin D Depletors: Mineral oil, smog, barbiturates, prednisone, Dilantin, sleeping pills, cortisone, anticonvulsant.

Vitamin E (Tocopherol)

Fat soluble—small amounts stored in liver and fatty acids.

Principal Sources: Wheat germ, lettuce, watercress, spinach, oats, corn, green peas, most green leafy vegetables, vegetable oils, peanut oil. Herbs: alfalfa, blue cohosh, dulse, kelp, dong quai, eyebright, spirulina, ginseng, skullcap.

Function: Vitamins A and E activate each other. Alpha-tocopherol is the most potent form of vitamin E. It is necessary for the body's effective use of linoleic acid and for the health of adrenal and pituitary glands. Vitamin E enhances the oxygenation of blood, reduces cholesterol, increases fertility and male potency, and revitalizes and strengthens heart muscles. Selenium increases the power of vitamin E, thus helping to strengthen and tone up muscles, protect lungs, retard cancer, prevent sterility, and protect against radiation.

Therapeutic Uses: Healing scar tissue, burns, aging, blood clots, heart failure repair, diuretic, blood pressure, migraines, headaches, muscular dystrophy, cold sores, coronary thrombosis, nephritis, miscarriage.

Vitamin E Depletors: Estrogen, birth control pills, chlorine, mineral oil, heat, food processing, inorganic iron, rancid fat.

Vitamin F (Unsaturated Fatty Acids)

Fat soluble—small amount stored in liver.

Principal Sources: Oats, rye, nuts, avocado, all unsaturated vegetable oils. Herbs: alfalfa, Irish moss.

Function: This vitamin is beneficial to the adrenal and thyroid glands and helps with blood coagulation and the growth and respiration of organs. It contributes to healthy hair and skin, and maintaining reliance and lubrication of all cells. Vitamin F stimulates the conversion of carotene into the form of vitamin A. It also provides some protection against the effects of X-rays and is best absorbed with vitamin E.

Therapeutic Uses: Cholesterol, hardening of the arteries, blood pressure, colitis, diabetes, allergies, diarrhea, eczema, gallstones, varicose veins, nail problems, asthma, multiple sclerosis, arthritis, acne, constipation, dermatitis, common cold, and obesity.

Vitamin F Depletors: Radiation, X-rays, heat, oxygen, rancid oils, unsaturated fats.

Vitamin H (Biotin)

Water soluble—stored in liver.

Principal Sources: Brewer's yeast, wheat germ, sprouts, molasses. Herbs: alfalfa, barberry.

Function: Biotin participates in the normal growth of all body tissues and cells, therefore, it is needed especially during pregnancy and lactation. It regulates the metabolism of carbohydrates, fat, protein, and utilization of B-complex vitamins. It helps to maintain skin, hair, all secreting glands, nerves, bone marrow, male sex hormones, and fatty acid production.

Therapeutic Uses: Baldness, mental depression, dermatitis, eczema, leg cramps, digestion.

Vitamin H Depletors: Process of refinement as in modern cereals, antibiotics, mineral oil, raw egg whites, sulfa drugs, alcohol, estrogen, sugar.

Vitamin K

Fat soluble—small amount stored in liver.

Principal Sources: Soybeans, green leafy vegetables, whole grains, legumes. Herbs: alfalfa, corn silk, Irish moss, kelp, sheperd's purse.

Function: Vitamin K is necessary for the formation of prothrombin (a blood-clotting chemical) and is produced in the intestines of well-nourished individuals. It is important for normal function of the heart and liver and needs bile to be utilized. K also protects the liver against lead pollution. In addition, it assists in the conversion of carbohydrates into glucose and will prevent hemorrhaging after surgical operations.

Therapeutic Uses: Antihemorrhagic, excessive menstrual flow, colitis, bruises, preparation for childbirth, gallstones, coronary thrombosis. Natural vitamin K is nontoxic. Synthetic can be toxic, not more than 300 to 500 micrograms recommended.

Vitamin P (Bioflavonoid)

Principal Sources: Citrus fruit pulp, grapes, black currants, prunes, spinach, buckwheat. Herbs: paprika, black currants, rose hips.

Function: Bioflavonoid increases the effectiveness of vitamin C, which builds the immune system. Vitamin P prevents and heals bleeding gums and stops capillary bleeding, increases anti-inflammatory activity, and is a natural diuretic.

Therapeutic Uses: Colds, scurvy, rheumatism, varicose veins, pneumonia, asthma, ulcers, hemorrhoids, edema, postpartum bleeding, cataracts, hypertension, respiratory infection, allergies, wound healing, viral infections, duodenal ulcers, spontaneous abortion, hemophilia, leukemia.

Vitamin P Depletors: Smoking, aspirin, alcohol, antibiotics, cortisone, pain-killers.

Vitamin T

Principal Sources: Sesame seeds, tahini.

Function: Although very little is known as yet on this new vitamin, researchers are aware that it does assist in normalizing blood coagulation and the forming of platelets. In addition, vitamin T may improve failing memory and poor concentration.

Therapeutic Uses: Anemia, hemophilia.

Vitamin U

Principal Sources: Found in cabbage juice, sauerkraut, and raw celery juice.

Function: This vitamin was only recently discovered, however, it has been found to be very high in chlorophyll, which is one of the best natural medicines available.

Therapeutic Uses: Duodenal and peptic ulcers.

Vitamin U Depletors: Heat.

MINERALS

Calcium

Principal Sources: Barley, kale, nuts, sesame seeds, unrefined grains. Herbs: alfalfa, barberry, bayberry, black cohosh, buchu, fennel, eyebright, dandelion, damiana, chamomile, chickweed, cascara sagrada, parsley, horsetail.

Function: Essential for smooth functioning of heart muscles and muscular movements of intestines (peristaltic action) aiding digestion. To function efficiently, calcium must be in combination with magnesium; phosphorus; vitamins A, C, and D; as well as zinc and inositol for proper absorption. It also must have acid, otherwise it will collect in joints and tissues. Necessary for the formation of bones and teeth and to maintain healthy glands. Only when calcium levels are low can a virus infection occur, improves acid-alkaline balance, metabolizes iron, helps vitamin-C function, protects against heavy metals and radioactive material.

Therapeutic Uses: Anemia, hemophilia, healing of bones,

wounds, acne, scrofula, stress, hypoglycemia, charlie horses, leg cramps, rickets, cardiovascular health, lowers cholesterol and triglycerides, aging, arthritis, asthma, hayfever, rheumatism, menstrual cramps, backache, sleeplessness, infections.

Calcium Depletors: Aspirin, chocolate, stress, lack of exercise, lack of magnesium, lack of hydrochloric acid, mineral oil, oxalic acid, phytic acid, high animal protein diet, tetracycline, table salt, excessive phosphorus.

Chlorine—Organic

Principal Sources: Rye flour. Herbs: alfalfa, barberry, kelp.

Function: Essential for the production of vital gastric juices aiding digestion, regulates heart action, and normalizes blood pressure, expels waste, purifies and disinfects, fights germs and bacteria, assists liver, rejuvenates all body's skin tissue, helps regulate acid, and alkaline balance of blood and hormone distribution.

Therapeutic Uses: Tetanus, intestinal colic, injuries, burns, restlessness, sluggish liver, breast lumps, swollen glands, skin itch and rashes, pyorrhea, catarrh.

Chlorine Depletors: High table salt level can give excess inorganic chlorine. Inorganic destroys vitamin E and intestinal flora.

Chromium

Principal Sources: Molasses, spices, whole-grain cereals, brewer's yeast. Herbs: kelp, spirulina.

Function: Essential for the metabolism of glucose for energy and synthesis of fatty acids, cholesterol, and protein; helps in blood sugar regulation; believed to help in the prevention of heart attacks.

Therapeutic Uses: Arteriosclerosis, diabetes, growth aid, hypoglycemia, pregnant women, high blood pressure, cholesterol level.

Chromium Depletors: Refined starches and carbohydrates, sugar.

Cobalt

Principal Sources: Sea vegetation, apricots. Herbs: dandelion, horsetail, kelp, red clover, spirulina.

Function: Essential for human nutrition aids in the assimilation and synthesis of vitamin B_{12}, stimulates many enzymes for the body. Essential in the building of red blood cells and in the maintenance and function of other cells. Cobalt must be supplied by the diet, increases assimilation of iron.

Therapeutic Uses: Pernicious anemia, nervous disorders, growth aid, heart palpitations.

Cobalt Depletors: Alcohol, sunlight, sleeping pills, estrogen.

Copper—Trace Mineral

Principal Sources: Whole-grain sources, almonds, green leafy vegetables, dried legumes, beans, blackstrap molasses. Herbs: burdock, chickweed, garlic, eyebright, juniper, kelp, spirulina.

Function: Copper is part of every body tissue, with manganese improves proper assimilation of iron and formation of red blood cells, RNA production, improves digestive system, involved in formation of myelin sheath (protective covering of nerve fiber), maintains muscle tone, converts amino acid tyrosine that gives color to skin and hair, synthesizes phospholipids, functions with vitamin C.

Therapeutic Uses: Anemia, osteoporosis, baldness, bedsores, edema, leukemia. An excess may cause arthritis.

Copper Depletors: Excessive zinc and molybdenum.

Fluorine—Organic

Principal Sources: Avocado, cabbage, garlic, oats, brown rice. Herbs: alfalfa, black walnut, hops, kelp, spirulina. Inorganic fluorine considered highly toxic.

Function: Called the decay-resistant element. Fluorine is essential for blood, spleen, tooth enamel, bones, skin, hair, nails, iris. Helps prevent curvature of the spine, diseases, reduces acidity of mouth which causes tooth decay. Fluorine and sodium are two elements that enable us to utilize calcium.

Therapeutic Uses: Flu, colds, eye problems, ulcers, nervousness, stress, falling hair, helps expectant mothers, parasites, varicose veins.

Fluorine Depletors: Cooking, heat, refined cereals impair absorption of fluorine.

Iodine

Principal Sources: Garlic, onions, eggplant, mushrooms, potatoes. Herbs: kelp, dulse, black walnut, spirulina.

Function: Essential for regulating the thyroid gland, manufacturing the hormone thyroxin to control the metabolism of the body, affecting growth rate, digestion, and burning up of excess fat. Regulates cholesterol levels, prevents cretinism in newborns when taken by pregnant women, essential in energy production, prevention of anemia, necessary for lymphatic system, protects against toxins in the brain.

Therapeutic Uses: Goiter, irregular heartbeat, hardening of the arteries, nervousness, irritability, obesity, low blood pressure, cretinism, angina pectoris, arterio and atherosclerosis, hyper- and hypothyroidism, arthritis, hair and skin problems, catarrh, breast cancer.

Iodine Depletors: Heat, food poisoning.

Iron—Organic

Principal Sources: Blackberries, cherries, dried fruits, strawberry juice, spinach greens, celery. Herbs: capsicum, butcher's-broom, horsetail, marshmallow, dulse, kelp, uva-ursi, sarsaparilla, golden seal, fenugreek, echinacea, dong quai, dandelion.

Function: Called the anti-anemia mineral. Calcium and copper needed for effective iron absorption, and combined with protein forms hemoglobin; improves protein metabolism; needed to bring oxygen to the lungs and to all the body's muscular cells; improves circulation; intensifies mental vitality, liver, kidney, and heart function, digestion, and elimination. Iron and oxygen promote youthfulness.

Therapeutic Uses: Dizziness, depression, headaches, anemia, heartburn, breathing difficulty, heart palpitations, alcoholism, constipation, colitis, menstruation, colds, sore throat, wound healing, diabetes, peptic ulcer, nephritis.

Overdose agitates body functions. An inorganic iron test on mice proved fatal.

Iron Depletors: Phosphates, food additives, food preservatives, EDTA, tea and coffee, excessive phosphorus, manganese.

Magnesium

Principal Sources: Unpolished rices, wheat germ, almonds, avocados, whole grains, greens, berries, grapefruits, barley. Herbs: kelp, valerian, stevia, skullcap, red raspberry, gotu kola, red clover, papaya, oatstraw, mullein, marshmallow, horsetail, fennel, eyebright, spirulina, peach bark, chickweed.

Function: Called the anti-stress mineral. Assists in the absorption of calcium, phosphorus, sodium, potassium, B complex, C, and E. Essential for formation of strong bones, teeth, lungs, and all body tissues; calms nerves; promotes sleep, proper digestion; nourishes the white nerve fiber of the brain and spinal cord; protects against heart attacks; activator of enzymes, in the use of proteins and vitamins.

Therapeutic Uses: Alcoholism, kidney stones, arthritis, hardening of the arteries, high blood pressure, osteoporosis, leukemia, neuritis, pain prevention, memory, senility, irritability, acidity, sinusitis, stiff muscles, neuralgia, convulsions. Large amounts may be toxic. Check with your health care professional or nutritionist.

Magnesium Depletors: Alcohol, synthetic vitamin D in excess, diuretics, coffee, tobacco, refined sugar, digitalis.

Manganese—Trace Mineral

Principal Sources: Nuts, seeds, avocados, barley, kidney beans, leaf lettuce, grapefruit, apricots. Herbs: eyebright, spirulina, sarsaparilla, red raspberry, ginger, gotu kola, catnip, chickweed, bilberry, black walnut, blue cohosh, buchu, uva-ursi.

Function: Essential for the proper function of the pituitary gland as well as the healthy functioning of all the body's glands. Manganese is a brain and nerve food element stored in combination with lecithin, required for the formation of red blood cells, regulates menstrual period, essential for expectant mothers and during lactation, good memory builder, essential for protein and carbohydrate metabolism, especially for sex hormones, and improves eyesight.

Therapeutic Uses: Diabetes, asthma, muscular and mental fatigue, epilepsy, and digestion.

Manganese Depletors: Large phosphorus and calcium intake, also high iron intake.

Molybdenum

Principal Sources: Buckwheat, leafy dark green vegetables, lima beans, barley, wheat germ.

Function: Essential for enzyme actions, believed to help prevent esophageal cancer and dental caries. Frees iron stored in liver, carries oxygen to body cells and tissues, helps eliminate toxic nitrogen waste.

Therapeutic Uses: Anemia.

Molybdenum Depletors: Copper and refined foods.

Phosphorus

Principal Sources: Barley, beans, lentils, rice bran, dark green leafy vegetables, pumpkin seeds, nuts. Herbs: alfalfa, bilberry, garlic, oatstraw, peach bark, chickweed, burdock, horsetail, fennel.

Function: Vitamin D and calcium essential for proper phosphorus functioning. Phosphorus essential for cell division and reproduction, promotes secretion of hormones and maintenance and repair of entire system; stimulates blood circulation; keeps acid out of bloodstream; provides quick release of energy; utilization of fast proteins, carbohydrates; reduces possibility of cancerous tissue formation; assists transfer of fatty acids through the body; normalizes blood pressure.

Therapeutic Uses: Blood pressure, arthritis, brain, tooth and gum disorders, backache, sterility, impotence, anti-aging, equilibrium and coordination of muscles.

Phosphorus Depletors: Sugar; excess intake of aluminum, magnesium, and iron; salts from cookware; mineral oil; tobacco.

Potassium

Principal Sources: Bananas, beans, almonds, and whole grains. Herbs: dulse, kelp, Irish moss, valerian, stevia, skullcap, sage, sarsaparilla, safflower, red clover, ginger, peach bark, peppermint, parsley, horsetail, hops, and garlic.

Function: Potassium is a healing mineral. It works together with sodium to keep a good acid-alkaline balance. Potassium also assists with the body's regenerative powers and strengthens the heart muscles. It helps to change glycogen to glucose, aids in waste elimination, and repairs the liver.

Therapeutic Uses: Useful for physical and mental stress and fights the hardening of the arteries; beneficial for rheumatism, arthritis, heart problems, high blood pressure, and diabetes.

Potassium Depletors: Cooking and processing; alcohol; coffee; diuretics; laxatives; cortisone; excess salt, sugar, and heat.

Selenium

Principal Sources: Bran, whole grains, brazil nuts, broccoli, onions, tomatoes, asparagus, mushrooms. Herbs: black walnut, horsetail, hawthorn berries, aloe vera, spirulina, slippery elm, ginseng, red raspberry, pau d'arco, marshmallow, chaparral, catnip, black cohosh, blessed thistle, blue cohosh, buchu.

Function: Selenium works with vitamin E as an antioxidant of toxic materials and helps the body make use of oxygen. It is also good for the prevention of chromosomal breakage which causes birth defects. Selenium is thought to be good in the prevention of breast cancer. In addition, it delays the oxidation of polyunsaturated fatty acids, which provides elasticity of all skin tissues.

Therapeutic Uses: Helps fight premature aging, scalp problems, emphysema, high blood pressure, and infertility.

Selenium Depletors: High fat intake, stress.

Silicon

Principal Sources: Oats, barley, nuts, seeds, cereals, grains, rice polishings, concentrated in the outer skin layer of fresh fruits and vegetables. Herbs: oatstraw, eyebright, echinacea, corn silk, chickweed, skullcap, horsetail, gotu kola, golden seal, alfalfa, burdock.

Function: Fluorine is a necessary element for the effective use of silicon. Silicon is essential for healthy hair, skin, and teeth. It increases the alkalinity of the body and acts as a cleansing mineral. Silicon is good for proper circulation and protects against the development of cancer tissue. It also increases the body's vigor, energy, strength, and resistance.

Therapeutic Uses: Helps fight mental fatigue, baldness, nervousness, exhaustion, poor vision, and insomnia.

Silicon Depletors: Fats, starches, and sugar.

Sodium

Principal Sources: Black mission figs, okra, celery, and watercress. Herbs: alfalfa, chickweed, buchu, burdock, gotu kola, safflower, sarsaparilla, rose hips, peppermint, papaya, parsley, dandelion.

Function: Sodium is only valuable when it is organic and balanced. It is essential for the production of saliva used for the digestion of all carbohydrates. It helps keep calcium in the body, prevents arthritis and excess mucus. Sodium is the main constituent of the

lymphatic system and assists in the elimination of carbon dioxide waste from the lungs. Along with potassium, it works to control the flow of substances in and out of each cell.

Therapeutic Uses: Aids in digestion; counters intestinal gas, neuralgia, rheumatism, and gout.

Sodium Depletors: Diarrhea, exercise, hot climate, excess sweating and vomiting.

Note: When sodium is inorganic (table salt), it is harmful to the kidneys and causes high blood pressure.

Sulphur

Principal Sources: Kale, cabbage, cauliflower, horseradish, Brussels sprouts, watercress, chervil, parsley, celery, dried beans, and nuts. Herbs: alfalfa, kelp, mullein, barberry.

Function: Sulphur promotes growth, keeps hair glossy and the complexion clear. It works with the B-complex vitamins and acts as an oxidizing agent. It is essential for protein absorption. Sulphur contributes to the normal functioning of the heart muscles and must be balanced with phosphorus. It is responsible for the metabolism of carbohydrates and promotes bile secretion, regulates nerve impulses, and stimulates egg and sperm production.

Therapeutic Uses: Sulphur is useful for proper digestion and the purification of the blood. It helps fight diseases, including hepatitis, dandruff, acne, and depression. This mineral helps maintain healthy hair, skin, and nails while also balancing the menstrual cycle.

Sulphur Depletors: Cooking.

Vanadium

Principal Sources: Soybeans, air. Herbs: kelp.

Function: This mineral is good for the circulation and the prevention of excessive cholesterol deposits in the blood vessels and central nervous system. Vanadium is essential for the metabolism of iron and helps with bones, cartilage, and teeth.

Therapeutic Uses: Vanadium is good at fighting tooth decay, high cholesterol levels, and heart attacks.

Vanadium Depletors: Food processing.

Zinc

Principal Sources: Whole-grain cereals, wheat germ, wheat bran, pumpkin seeds, avocado, and asparagus. Herbs: capsicum, spirulina, psyllium, garlic, sage, butcher's-broom, lady's slipper, eyebright, echinacea, bilberry, buchu, gotu kola.

Function: Zinc is essential for the growth of bones and teeth. It is one of the main healing minerals for healthy hair and for the proper digestion of proteins and carbohydrates. Zinc contributes to the use of insulin and is necessary for the health of the prostate gland. It helps the body manufacture various male hormones and is needed for the metabolism of B-complex vitamins.

Therapeutic Uses: Helps to fight atherosclerosis, sterility, and heart attacks as well as ulcers, acne, and dermatitis; increases the body's resistance to infection and aids in the acid-alkaline balance.

Zinc Depletors: Excessive calcium, antacids, alcohol, and oral contraceptives.

INDEX

In Conclusion

Dear Friend:

We at Delights of the Garden are honored by the fact that you have chosen to share in the fruits of our labors. We humbly thank you for taking time and energy to read our book. "The journey of a thousand miles begins with the first step." It is our hope that this book can be the first step for you in a personal journey toward optimal health.

I know that the tone of the book is a little bit harsh at times, especially when I'm arguing the case for vegetarianism. This is done intentionally—to make a strong impression. We have a lot of work to do if we are to counteract the years of schooling that taught us that it was absolutely necessary to eat animals in order to live. Through decades of socialization we have come to attach strong emotional feelings to many of the foods we eat and even to the very act of eating itself. Today, we eat more out of habit than out of actual hunger. We eat because it is a particular time of day or because we are attending a particular event. Ultimately we come to associate certain foods with good times, exciting places, and pleasant gatherings of friends and family.

Fortunately *for humanity,* we continue to get a second chance with our children. We have the chance to create what I call "food-experiences" for children. Instead of them associating hot dogs and hamburgers with fun birthday parties, we can create environments where they make the same association with, say, "veggie tuna!" Sounds wild? But it can easily happen. If you feel that you, personally, could never—or would never want to—give up meat, consider this: Your child's taste buds are clean slates, waiting to be written on. They have no "acquired tastes"!

What the world needs now is true education. The Latin root of the word *education* means to bring from within out. This implies that we have all that we need inside of us. When we understand this we will begin to truly educate ourselves. We will learn to *listen* to our bodies and to treat them like the priceless gifts that they are.

Peace and Blessings,

Imar Hutchins